"This book will lead you on a journey that is real and raw and inspiring. Cindy skillfully retraces her steps as she escorts you down the path that God chose for her family. Through her trusting eyes you will experience the profound peace that He provides – even in the most difficult times. Anyone who meets Cindy through her music, her speaking, and now her book, will be impacted by her quiet strength!"

~ Gwen Diaz ~ Author, Speaker, Ministry Leader, Mother of 4 boys

"As I read Quiet Strength, I was awestruck by Cindy's unparalleled honesty, courage, and faith. There were moments in this book that made me laugh like I was sitting with an old friend and there were moments that took my breath away because I was so overwhelmed with grief for this family. In the end, I read it in one sitting because I couldn't stand to walk away without knowing 'what comes next.' Cindy's quiet strength is an inspiration to us all!"

~ Emma Reynolds ~ Divisional Field Director for Stonecroft, Worship Leader

"As one of Cindy's best friends, I have been privileged to watch and actually experience with Cindy the stories you are about to read. As you are captivated by Cindy's life story, you will experience her deep trust in God's goodness even in the midst of extreme trials. Cindy and Casey have lived their authentic faith out loud, and the Lord continues to bless their marriage, family, and ministry. Cindy shows us all that praising God is more than a feeling—it is a choice. This truth is not only evident in the pages of Quiet Strength, it is evident in the way Cindy lives each and every day!"

~ Angela Batterman ~ Worship Leader, Music Educator

"This book is a strong testimony of faith and trust. I am awed by the power of our heavenly Father to inspire this wonderful work. The living words of scripture throughout are so healing. I am encouraged by Cindy and Casey's amazing faith in the midst of many devastating trials. This book will be extremely helpful to all who read it."

~ Bonnie Allen ~ Musician, Ministry Leader

QUIET STRENGTH

A TRUE STORY OF UNEXPECTED LOSS
AND UNEXPLAINABLE PEACE

CINDY LOU CLEVELAND

CLEVELAND CREATIVE PRODUCTIONS
LAKELAND, FLORIDA, U.S.A.®

ISBN: 9781700959188
Library of Congress Control Number: 201991694

Published by Cleveland Creative Productions®

www.CindyLouCleveland.com

To Casey ~
who has given me stories to write about.
To Solomon ~
who has always been tender toward my tears.
To Isaac ~
who has enriched my life by richly living yours.
To Daniel ~
who has been instrumental in the healing of my heart.
To Josiah ~
who has endless hugs and sweetness galore.
To Selah ~
who has a special place in my heart and, someday,
in my arms.

THE SECRET [OF THE SWEET, SATISFYING COMPANIONSHIP] OF THE LORD

HAVE THEY WHO FEAR (REVERE AND WORSHIP) HIM, AND HE WILL SHOW

THEM HIS COVENANT AND REVEAL TO THEM ITS [DEEP, INNER] MEANING.

PSALM 25:14 (AMPCE)

April,

You are a

blessing!

Contents

FOREWORD

One Sunday morning I shared with my congregation the news that five of our loved and cherished members had died that week. You could hear the gasps in the
congregation. This was hard news. When the worship
service ended a member of the congregation quickly
hurried to me, placed her hands on my shoulders and
said, "This is terrible, having so many key people die in
one week. What are we going to do? How do you do
this?" That last question has never left me. Again and
again we are challenged by the realities of life and ask,
"How will I do this? Can I do this?"

I have learned that change can bring stress. A
move, a job change, the birth of a child, a new relationship, while often exciting and wonderful, also bring the
stressors which accompany change. Even more stress is
brought by difficult, heartbreaking situations. Most of
us are challenged by one painful situation, but what if
the pain comes again and again? "How will you do
this?"

Cindy and Casey Cleveland have asked this question, among many others, many times. Life was wonderful, going well, encouraging and hopeful when the
bottom began to erode and eventually fell out, not once,
but again and again. Within a few short years, their
lives began to look like a chapter from the book of Job.
There seemed to be no time to heal from one loss before

11

the next one struck. Just one of the heartbreaking events would overwhelm most people. The losses were personal and crushing.

Yet, Cindy and Casey found that what God has promised is an important reality. They saw through their pain and tears that what the Psalmist declares is a needed anchor, "Even though I walk through the darkest valley, I will fear no evil, for you are with me" (Psalm 23:4 NIV). The Clevelands found themselves at the point where they had to decide if they really believed this promise. It is easy to claim faith when all is going well, but for them the deep, awful, heart breaking realities would not allow lip service. They had to decide if they really believed. Cindy writes, "In the days, weeks, and months ahead tears would flow—sometimes unexpectedly, sometimes uncontrollably. In reality, I felt like a chunk of my heart had been ripped from my chest. I knew I needed time to heal from this deep inner pain. And somehow I knew my heart would heal over time in the comforting arms of Jesus."

Those wonderful words, "...in the comforting arms of Jesus," are more than a metaphor. These are the arms Cindy and Casey lean on every day, every hour, every moment. In *Quiet Strength*, Cindy opens her heart, sharing the pain, hopes, and healing which have been part of her journey with Casey. It is her story, but it speaks to our stories. It addresses the question, "how will I do this?" *Quiet Strength* doesn't offer answers, it offers relationship—relationship and embrace by the God of love. In that relationship is a reminder that dealing with pain and loss is not meant to be borne alone. Rather, God is with us. God holds us and journeys through the dark valley. God's presence is a quiet and powerful strength, given to us so we "are able to do this."

Rev. David McEntire, Senior Pastor
First United Methodist Church
Lakeland, Florida

14

ACKNOWLEDGEMENTS

With heartfelt thanks:

To *anyone and everyone* who has said a prayer for me or my family. Your prayers have sustained us and led us to the writing of this book. For you all, I am forever grateful.

To the most consistent prayer warrior I know, my mom ~ *Ann Pike*. Your daily prayers for every family member by name have made an eternal impact that we have yet to fully realize. You are the woman whom I aspire to be and the person to whom I attribute saving Casey's life. For you, I am forever grateful.

To my dad ~ *Don Pike* ~ whose daily life taught me perseverance and showed me how to "be a good example." Your constant love and teddy bear hugs have meant more to me than you will ever know. For you, I am forever grateful.

To my five siblings ~ *Dave, Connie, Doug, Greg, and Cathy* ~ who have known me my whole life. You have seen me at my best and loved me through my worst. And who would have thought your baby sister would write a book?! For you, and your families, I am forever grateful.

To my other parents ~ *Gary and Tee Cleveland*. Some might call you my in-laws. I prefer to call you Dad and Mom. Thank you for raising your son Casey to be the man I will always love. Thank you for loving and supporting us in ways beyond what I ever expected, yet obviously needed. Your constant care and personal sacrifice are beautiful and humbling. For you both, I am forever grateful.

To *Rhea Cleveland.* Thank you for being a devoted sister to Casey and a fun friend to us all. You provide frequent laughs, and not-so-frequent hugs. Yet for every hug—and for you—I am forever grateful.

To *Virginia Furman.* You are our only grandparent left here with us on this earth. For 95 years, you have lived and loved well. For you, I am forever grateful.

To *Angela Batterman,* my forever friend. Over the years, across the miles, through the exhilarating highs and the devastating lows, you remain my friend—constant, true, faithful. Plus, you're the one responsible for Casey and me dating in the first place! For you, I am forever grateful.

To *Gerry Hubbs (a.k.a. Miss GG).* Your friendship is sweet to my soul. Oh the memories we share—from worship nights, to funeral services, to late night conversations, to hunkering down during hurricanes! You will always be a part of the Cleveland clan. For you, I am forever grateful.

To "Erika the Editor." *Erika Mathews,* you are a jewel. Although our only correspondence has been through word documents and emails, I definitely feel a sweet spirit connection with you. Thank you for all you have done to enhance the effectiveness of this book's message. What a delight you are! For you, I am forever grateful.

To *Allen Cleveland*, proofreader extraordinaire. Although we share the same last name, our eight cousin, twice removed status keeps us from attending the same family reunions. That's why I was thrilled when our paths crossed again and you agreed to take on this challenge. You are amazing at your craft. For you, I am forever grateful.

To *David McEntire*, pastor, supporter, believer, friend. Thank you for your love and support throughout this journey. Your voice has been a constant stream of peace and encouragement. Thank you for agreeing to write the Foreword for this book and reminding us of the "quiet and powerful strength, given to us so we 'are able to do this.'" For you, I am forever grateful.

To *Mark and Emma Reynolds*. Although the Lord has moved you away from us physically, you remain close to our hearts and your friendship is dear to both Casey and me. For you both, we are forever grateful.

To so many others: *Gwen Diaz*, for being my role model and prayer support. *Bonnie Allen*, for always believing in me and encouraging me. *Kayla Tirrell*, for answering all my nagging indie author questions. *Charles*

Asbridge, for the friendship that brought us so close and for loving your kids well. *Randy Hardy*, for remaining a true friend to Casey over the years and through the changes. For you all, I am forever grateful.

To *Hillcrest Coffee*, for providing the calming, yet inspiring, environment where a book can be written. Several mornings a week, I would find myself in the back corner in the back room, writing and healing. Thank you for the beautiful space. For you—*Brian Goding and your staff*—I am forever grateful.

To the *church and school communities* in Lakeland (and elsewhere) that have shaped us and supported us: Victory Church, First Presbyterian Church, Presbyterian Church in the Highlands, Life Church, Word of Faith Family Church (Daytona Beach/Orlando), Shepherd's Community United Methodist Church, Lakeside Baptist Church, First United Methodist Church, Joyful Hearts Preschool, Little Shepherd's Preschool, Classical Conversations (Lakeland/Daytona Beach), First Methodist School (Bartow), Lakeland Christian School. For you all, we all are forever grateful.

To *my sweet, sweet boys*. You will never fully know the joy you bring to my life. Your hugs, your prayers, your "I love you's" are more precious to me than anything money can buy. You are my treasure. I am so glad God chose me to be your mommy. For you—*Solomon, Isaac, Daniel, Josiah*—I am eternally grateful.

To *Casey*, the love of my life, my best friend, my hero. Your continual reminder that I was the only one who could write this story has made this book a reality. Thank you for being my #1 cheerleader. Thank you for believing in me when I forgot how to believe in myself. Thank you for leading our family well and for keeping our focus on what really matters. For you, I am eternally grateful.

To *Daddy God*, who has given me a story worthy to be written. Thank You for never leaving or forsaking me. Thank You for the measure of faith You have given me to believe that regardless of our circumstances, You are still good, You are still faithful, and You are still worthy of our praise. For You, forever and eternally, I am grateful.

INTRODUCTION

As I travel and speak, I share a story—my story, written here in the pages of Quiet Strength. Yet, following each speaking engagement, I am reminded that everyone has a story. Some of our stories are perfectly pretty, but for most of us, our stories are marvelously messy.

In the first three decades of my life, my story was pretty—even picturesque. I grew up in a stable family where love was prominent. I received a quality education, followed by good jobs and exciting opportunities. I had everything I needed and most of what I wanted.

Then came 2007....

Then came 2009....

Then came 2011....

Then came 2014....

With one heartbreak following another, life was messy. Yet, in the disarray, I began to see something.

Something marvelous. Something meaningful.

Quiet Strength is not a "how-to" book, but it is a "how I" book.

~ *How I* discovered purpose in the midst of my pain.
~ *How I* clung to God and His word for strength each day.
~ *How I* chose to become better instead of bitter.

As you read my story, I hope you see *your* story.
~ Your story full of purpose even in the pain.
~ Your story full of hope even in the most devastating circumstances.
~ Your story full of healing even with a wounded heart.

Together let's begin our journey as we discover the source of quiet strength.

24

QUIET STRENGTH WHILE WAITING

~ WHEN'S THE GREEN LIGHT?

No earthly eye would have ever matched the stylish beauty pageant girl with the long-haired voice performance major wearing raggedy jeans. Yet under a heavenly hand, I met the love of my life during our freshman year at Florida Southern College in Lakeland, Florida, my hometown. While Casey majored in voice performance, I studied for a degree in music education with emphasis on voice. Due to our striking differences, we had no attraction to each other at first. Following in the footsteps of my beautiful older sister Cathy, I pursued beauty pageants. This meant I exercised every day, ate very little fat, and constantly dressed classy. Casey, on the other hand, was not the exercising or stylish type. Dr. Pepper®, long hair, and worn-out jeans comprised his signature look.

During our sophomore year, Casey and I were both involved in other relationships. At this time, a friendship started to develop between Casey and me. After the guy I was dating broke up with me, Casey asked my best friend Angela if this guy had hurt me. Although I was saddened by the breakup, I was not hurt by my previous boyfriend. Yet, Casey's concern for me showed a sweet, tender side of his personality that I would eventually find to be very attractive.

That summer, once his previous relationship had also dissolved, Casey started to pursue me gently. A postcard while he was traveling, a phone call when he returned, a casual car-shopping outing...that type of pursuit.

When our junior year began, my friend Angela encouraged me to talk to Casey about his intentions with our relationship. As I walked to my dorm room after classes one day, I noticed Casey sitting by himself. Angela's encouragement ran through my head. I remember praying as I turned around to talk to him, "Okay, Lord, do with this whatever You want." Little did I know at that moment that I would be spending the rest of my life with this amazing guy.

So I approached Casey, and completely uncharacteristic of my personality, the words flowed from my mouth. "So Casey, what do you want with me?"

I'm sure he was shocked! I don't remember the specifics of the conversation, but I do believe he expressed his interest in pursuing a dating relationship with me. Oh boy! Where was this going? I didn't see Casey as being "my type," yet I found myself intrigued by him and interested in seeing where this relationship would go.

The next weekend, he invited me to the elegant Columbia Restaurant on St. Petersburg Pier. My understanding was that the college and career group from his church would be present, and I even cancelled plans to go to a Harry Connick Jr. concert so I could go out with Casey on September 16, 1994. Torrents of rain obscured our vision during the entire drive, so it was no surprise that none of the college or career friends showed up to dinner in St. Pete.

It was a delightful dinner, just the two of us. Our server, Dallas, served with politeness and attentiveness throughout the meal, and we enjoyed a decadent dessert. At dinner, Casey informed me that he had something for me that night—some sort of surprise, I presumed.

As we left St. Pete, Casey wanted to take me to his old stomping grounds at Bradenton Beach. We took the long way, which just meant we had more time together. On the beach, Casey pulled out his guitar and sang a song he had written for me with lyrics that say, "Don't you ever stray away from me." It's a beautiful song and it was a very kind, bold gesture on our first date. Following the song were a walk on the beach, handholding, and a kiss while leaning against the volleyball pole.

When I first met Casey, I didn't think he was my type, but as I got to know him, I realized that he had so much more than what I was looking for in a life partner. My list of qualities in my future husband included important things like "being a spiritual leader," but my list contained other trivial characteristics such as "tall, dark, and handsome." Casey had so many qualities that I loved but didn't even know I wanted in a husband. He was humorous, creative, decisive, discerning, and sensitive to God's timing.

I'm not quite sure why, but as soon as I graduated from FSC, my feelings toward Casey started to change. I broke up with him, breaking his heart. During this time apart, I had the opportunity to pursue a relationship with a guy I had always compared Casey to—only to find out that this guy was not all I had made him out to be.

Throughout my dating years I felt unfulfilled without a boyfriend, yet I always wanted to be content with only Jesus. This was the time God granted me to discover complete fulfillment within Him. And I'm so grateful to be able to say that happened. By His grace, I truly was fulfilled with Christ alone.

Yet, perhaps ironically, or perhaps due to the leading of God, during this time I realized I missed Casey's friendship.

My friend Angela, now a worship leader at a local

church, was putting together a brand-new band. Five months after our breakup, Casey and I were both asked to sing in this band. Since I knew we would be seeing each other on a weekly basis, I thought Casey and I should get together to talk, so it wouldn't be so awkward at the church service. He agreed. We shared a fun outing to Orlando in my brand-new car that I wanted to show off to him. We had a great time, sharing life and laughs together again.

When I broke up with Casey, I knew I had hurt both him and myself. I also knew that if we were to get back together, I wanted the confidence of knowing this relationship would last because I didn't want to hurt either of us in that way again.

On October 11, 1996, we "kissed and made up." Yet three years passed before Casey would ask for my hand in marriage. During those years, Casey, his best friend Tom Carter, and the third male voice, Jason Seger, started a Christian band called Cleveland Carter. I was the keyboardist for the band, and over the years Casey and I enjoyed our travels with Cleveland Carter. As the band gained momentum, Casey's dad served as one of our drummers. We recorded albums and toured the eastern United States, hoping to be signed by a Christian label. I greatly enjoyed the travel and the music as well as the time with Casey.

Since Casey and I knew we wanted to marry, I kept waiting—somewhat patiently—for his proposal.

He kept waiting for God to give him the green light.

At last, Casey started his first full-time job. The very next day, his sweet proposal included the song he had written for and sung to me on our first date five years prior. Six months later we were married!

By the time Casey proposed to me, my family had grown to love him and were excited about our union. Yet the waiting process proved to be difficult for both of us. Other friends who had dated for much shorter time periods were marrying around us. It was challenging keeping ourselves sexually pure for five and a half years until our wedding night.

Looking back, I realize the waiting time truly strengthened our relationship and helped develop the love and commitment needed to help us stay loyal through our marriage relationship:

for better, for worse,
for richer, for poorer,
in sickness and in health,
to love and to cherish for as long as we both shall live.

QUIET STRENGTH IN BLESSINGS
~ CRAZY GOOD

Saturday, April 15, 2000, the day I had been dreaming about my whole life, finally arrived…my wedding day! Besides not sleeping much the night before—due to excitement, I'm sure (and the fact I couldn't find the CDs that had our songs we were going to dance to at our reception)—I was pumped and ready for the day. It's probably a good thing I didn't know Casey and his band buddies drove to Tampa to buy some sort of sound equipment…on our wedding day!

We dodged a light rain while getting my crinoline-lined wedding dress into the limousine that shuttled me and my bridesmaids to the church building. My parents escorted me down the aisle to see my soon-to-be husband and his parents, while the organist played the wedding processional. Casey was so handsome, and I was so excited to be marrying him.

We took many pictures prior to the service, and then it was time for all the guests to arrive. I loved sharing this special day with so many of our amazing family and friends. The forty-five-minute wedding ceremony went without a hitch. The music, the message, the vows, our first communion together as a married couple—all of it was just how I had pictured it and more. The only glitch I recall was finding out after the fact the Casey and I used the wrong candles for the unity candle...not a big deal, since the meaning of the unity of our families was in our hearts.

When it was time to kiss the bride, Casey turned to his audience and gave me a kiss worth remembering. We processed out with such joy and, after more pictures, loaded the limo to go to the reception.

Red and white roses were everywhere: on the tables, on the cake—everywhere. Dinner was delicious, the toasts were hilarious (with Casey's sister Rhea sharing a story about Casey and a spider—yikes!), the cakes were amazing, and the dances were so much fun! After hours of good, clean fun, it was time to leave. And guess what? More roses! Rose petals were thrown at us during our departure to the limo.

Casey and I anticipated that the limo driver would drive us off into the moonlight once we were safely in our seats in the back of the limo. But no...she was negotiating with my father about the $750.00

limousine bill! The delay made the departure a bit anti-climactic but certainly memorable and humorous. Now we could officially "make out," right? Well, no. Since this was prom weekend, limo drivers from all over the state were working that night. Our young lady was from Orlando, and since this was before GPS, she had no idea where she was going. So we spent the trip directing her to our hotel, which made for an unforgettable and comical ride.

Here we were, finally married and at our hotel—the newly renovated, historic Terrace Hotel in downtown Lakeland, Florida. As we approached our room, Casey picked me up, still in my wedding dress, and carried me over the threshold. So sweet! Once we were settled in our room, the first thing Casey led us to do was to get down on our knees, and he led us in a prayer together. What an awesome godly man I had just married! On that night, I was so glad I had saved myself for him.

Sunday morning was an early start since we were driving down to Miami to get on a cruise ship. I loved starting our marriage together in this way!

Our new life in Lakeland started out in a 900-square-foot duplex. It was perfect for us. Casey was working at Aluminum Inc., and I was teaching music to preschoolers as well as helping with the youth group at First Presbyterian Church. We were loving life together.

A year and a half into marriage, we were blessed to purchase our first house. It was a modest home, built in the 1950s, but we loved it. We developed strong relationships with new and old friends and even started exploring some new business opportunities. We were given a unique opportunity to travel with a choir to sing in Austria. Loving life and all the major blessings the Lord was pouring upon us, we were so overcome by our lives full of love, opportunities, and adventure that we didn't even consider that fact that our biggest blessings were still to come.

In September of 2004, Casey and I were working on developing new strategies and growth for one of our businesses, Cleveland School of Music. Shortly after, I discovered I was pregnant with our first child.

On Monday, June 13, 2005, our lives were forever blessed by the arrival of Solomon Lee Cleveland. It was not an easy delivery. Not only did I have a completely natural birth at a birthing center, he arrived weighing 10 pounds 2 ounces! I had to leave him to go to the hospital to be stitched up. By the time we finally got home later that day, I remember being so tired after being up for over twenty-four hours, yet I could not get my eyes off of this beautiful bundle. Solomon was such a gorgeous baby, and I was thrilled to be his mother.

We were loving life with our little one. What's more, we had Disney passes, so we could enjoy a day at Disney World anytime we wanted. Our family was blessed, our businesses were blessed, so it only seemed right to move into a dream home on Sugartree Drive.

This move happened while I was pregnant with our next biggest blessing, Isaac Lawrence Cleveland. He arrived on Saturday, March 24, 2007. I decided to be induced with him, so after checking in to the hospital that morning, I gave birth to our smallest child, weighing in at 8 pounds 3 ounces. He, too, was so beautiful and healthy, and my heart overflowed with all these blessings God was pouring into our lives. Indeed, life was crazy good.

Hines Photography

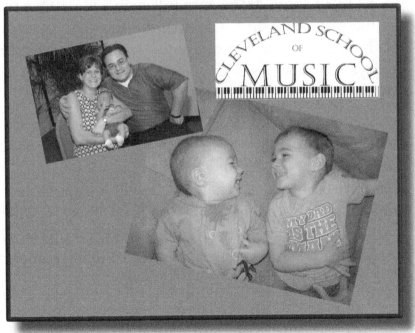

Quiet Strength of Trusting
~ Devastating Financial Blows

By the time 2007 was in full swing, we felt the pain of the real estate bust. Casey and a few of his buddies had recently become real estate investors, and we had enjoyed the benefits and comforts that came along with the boom.

But now life was different. 2007 brought with it challenges we had not previously experienced. In addition to our real estate business, we also owned Cleveland School of Music where we taught lessons to nearly one hundred students each week. Multiple teachers, staff, activities, and property were wrapped up into the business, and this season of financial challenges affected the school and brought us to a crossroads.

By the end of the year, I was offering a great deal of prayer regarding the future of CSM. I really wanted the school to continue, but I wasn't sure I could manage it effectively while still attempting to be a good wife and mother to two very young boys. One evening at the school, I experienced a wrestling prayer time with God. I sensed He wanted me to close the school, but I was seriously struggling with this decision. Yet I prayed, "Not my will, but Yours be done."

Although it was difficult, I found freedom in closing CSM. I felt God was blessing our obedience.

Yet even the blessings accompanying obedience still don't mean obedience is easy. In fact, our declining financial situation brought with it more stress and fear. Several of our properties trembled on the verge of foreclosure. When money did come in, we used it to buy food and to keep our dream home afloat.

Buying groceries was exhausting—not so much because I had two little ones accompanying me, but because each visit required a calculator in hand, knowing I didn't want to withdraw any more than the $35 that was currently in our bank account.

Our two vehicles were in repossession status, so most nights we kept one car in the garage and the other was "hiding" in the back yard behind a locked gate. One night the Lord woke me up just in time to walk to the stairwell window to see the tow truck backing into our driveway. My heart was pounding, wondering what would happen in the next few moments. Because neither car was accessible, the tow truck left, and I breathed a sigh of relief, thanking God for sparing us the inconvenience and humiliation of having our car repossessed.

By this point, November 2008 couldn't get here fast enough. That was the month the lease agreement expired on my fancy BMW that my loving husband gave to me as a birthday gift three years prior when life was booming. How much our lives had changed! We returned the car and began life with a single car that was soon paid off. Yay! No more repossession scares!

In the thick of these financial challenges, Casey and I chose to trust God at deeper levels than we had before. We leaned upon Him in the midst of our mess, and we found Him to be consistently faithful.

God demonstrated His goodness and faithfulness to us through the kindness of friends one weekend afternoon. The boys were napping, so Casey and I decided to rest as well. As we lay in the bed contemplating how empty our refrigerator was and what little funds we had to buy any food, we heard a knock on the door. A couple friends of ours stood outside holding bags of groceries. And I'm not talking just a couple bags—they made several trips to the car to get all the groceries in the house! These sweet friends, young in their faith (and I'm sure not overflowing in financial abundance), felt the Lord wanted them to buy these groceries for us, so they did. What a blessing this act of kindness was to us! Such encouragement on this dark, lonely road of financial uncertainty.

As much as we tried and prayed, the inevitable was happening: our primary residence—our dream home—threatened foreclosure. One evening we sought counsel from a friend who was money-savvy, and she questioned Casey and me about this "Goliath" we were facing. In I Samuel 17:37, before David slew Goliath, he singlehandedly killed a bear and a lion. Somehow Casey knew the financial challenges we had been facing for more than two years now were not a Goliath, but only a bear or a lion. Little did we know at that point the depth of trust we were developing in our faithful God as we faced this challenge. We would soon be relying upon Him even more deeply since Goliath was lurking around the corner.

QUIET STRENGTH OF PAIN
~ A CHUNK OF MY HEART IS RIPPED FROM MY CHEST

The belt of the treadmill fell away underfoot as the united chorus of Michael W. Smith's live worship album reverberated through my headphones. On that February morning in 2009, my imagination soared in the wonder of these hundreds of people unifying their voices and singing worship to God. In that moment, I sensed the Spirit of the Lord speak to my spirit. I felt Him say that He wanted me to have a community worship night. My first reaction was a simple, "Okay. That sounds cool."

Immediately, I started to get excited about the possibilities. Then I said, "Okay, Lord, when should we do this?"

To my surprise, the date April 25 popped into my mind. To my continued surprise, when I looked at the calendar, I discovered that April 25, 2009, was a Saturday! So I said, "Okay, Lord, let's do this!"

I started talking about the idea with close people in my life: Casey, my mom, my sister Cathy. I knew I would need their help and encouragement to be sure I would follow through with this event God told me to do.

The planning began, and the first Experience CommUNITY worship night was held on Saturday, April 25, 2009, in Branscomb Auditorium on the campus of Florida Southern College. It was a powerful night of worship through music, Scripture reading, drama, and dance. Over the course of the next couple years, six Experience CommUNITY worship nights would be held, which truly were community events, bringing together people of various denominations, races, and ages...just like Heaven is.

Yet I'm getting ahead of myself. Let's go back to February 2009.

That's when I found out I was pregnant again. Besides keeping up with two little boys, ages one and three, I was also exhausted from the pregnancy. Yet the planning of the first Experience CommUNITY was well on its way. By the time April 25 arrived, I was starting to show and starting to tell people about our growing family.

Since our financial situation was not good, I was accepted by Medicaid, and I started my prenatal care at the local birthing center. I was anticipating a due date around October 19, yet my ultrasound indicated a due date of November 9. It was a little bit of a shocker to realize I would be pregnant for an additional three weeks more than I originally anticipated, but the excitement of finding out I was pregnant with a girl overcame all other hesitancies.

Casey and I celebrated the news of a girl by having lunch together at Panera Bread. While there, we saw some ladies we knew from church. I was so excited to share the news with them, and I told them they were finding out this news even before we had told our parents.

How exciting it was to start imagining life with a little girl to raise, with two big brothers to help take care of her, with a father/daughter relationship to develop, and with the anticipation of many girly outings and activities in the years ahead! We were thrilled to contemplate welcoming our daughter into our home.

Since this season I'm writing about is full of hurt, let me take a moment to share a funny story that happened late in my pregnancy. I was about thirty-seven weeks along, and Casey and I made a stop at the local Dairy Queen. While I sat there enjoying my delicious treat with my very large baby bump, I noticed a little boy, about six years old, sitting with his dad. This little boy kept looking at me with the most confused and concerned look. He must have wondered why my tummy was so large. If I had felt comfortable enough with the father's reaction, I would have told this little guy that if you keep eating lots of ice cream, this tummy is what will happen to you!

I noticed when I went to bed on a Saturday night that I didn't remember feeling my baby move inside me, so I was very conscious of any movement on Sunday and the Monday morning of my due date. Since I couldn't recall any movement to speak of, I called the midwives, Melissa and Rebekah. Rebekah suggested I drink a cup of orange juice and then lie on my side for thirty minutes, and then let her know about any movements since the natural sugar in the orange juice should make the baby move. I wasn't sure if at times she was pushing up against the uterine wall or if it was the uterus contracting.

We made arrangements for my mom and me to meet Rebekah at the birthing center at 2:30 p.m. I went through my regular checkup. Rebekah asked if I was anxious at all. I truly was not. I was a little concerned since I hadn't felt her obviously move in a few days, but I was confident she was fine because God had spoken many things over my baby.

On January 10 of that year, a friend of great faith spoke from the Lord that I would give birth to a child. Then the Lord said through her, "Be strong." Just a few weeks later our baby girl was conceived. God also spoke that this child would be a helper, and that this would be an easy baby with an easy transition for the family.

About two weeks prior, a pastor-friend of ours mentioned that a family in their congregation had just lost a baby that was over twenty weeks along. She said she hated to share that with me since I was pregnant, too. I prayed for that family often, but I was not at all concerned for my baby because I knew God kept her safe. After all, we "abide in the shadow of the Almighty" (Psalm 91:1).

Rebekah started listening for my baby's heartbeat, and she couldn't find it with the Doppler fetal monitor. She searched and searched. Occasionally we would hear a heartbeat, but she confirmed that it was mine. I lay there and prayed quietly in my prayer language. Rebekah switched to another Doppler in case the first one was not working correctly. Still no heartbeat. She said to me, "You understand I should be able to hear the heartbeat, right?"

I understood. She said we would head over to the hospital for a sonogram. If no heartbeat was found, I would be induced. Rebekah asked if we wanted to pray together, so we all three lifted up a prayer.

That's when I called Casey. He was giving a guitar lesson to our nephew. Cathy's husband, Charles, was with Casey, so I knew Cathy would find out soon. Casey met us at the hospital, and we walked in together.

The doctor and team immediately got me undressed and started the sonogram on my baby. Once again, no heartbeat. Casey moved over to me, but he quickly became faint and had to sit down. He turned very white, so they gave him ammonia to sniff and a wet washcloth. He rapidly returned to normal.

Dr. Brenda Harris-Watson wanted to confirm her finding with a radiologist. The radiologist took several pictures on her machine. She confirmed no heartbeat and that the baby was in the transverse position—meaning her head was up on my left side, her back was down, and her legs were to my right side. Obviously, she could not be delivered in this position, so we were given the option of a C-section or of allowing Dr. Watson to try to move her into head-down position.

The staff left Casey and me alone to decide, and we chose to have Dr. Watson try to move baby into position. She explained that it would work or not, and she would try up to three times but would stop at any time if it was too uncomfortable for me. She also gave us her statistics, which were not encouraging: in her twenty-two years of practice, she had probably tried to move a baby from the transverse position twelve times and only been successful at three.

We had to wait for my blood work to return before the doctor would try to move the baby. That gave Casey and me time to pray and read Psalm 91. We were still very strongly believing that God would raise her up. We held on to that belief even after she was born. I thought it would be so great, especially after all the medical evidence that she was dead, for God to bring her back to life. In fact, I even prayed that if Jesus were in the room, I believe He would say, "She is only sleeping" like He said about Jairus' daughter in the Bible (see Luke 8:52).

I was very impressed with Casey in those moments because he said that if this does not turn out as we are believing, then there will be new guidelines on communication. We must not isolate ourselves, but we must communicate to one another what we are thinking. This is an ideal time for fear and the enemy's lies to take root, but we must talk about it. Already Casey was working to protect our marriage, and I deeply respect him for that!

Dr. Watson came in to move the baby into head-down position. She greased up my tummy and lifted up the baby's butt. At that moment, I prayed the doctor's hands would become God's hands and that He would move the baby into position. Sure enough, she (through God) moved her into position the first try! The three nurses in the room were very impressed. I knew the Lord's hand was involved, and now we were beginning to see His favor.

As they wheeled me down to the Labor and Delivery room, I asked if Marianne Power, the midwife who had delivered Solomon at the local birthing center and was now a full-time nurse at the hospital, was working tonight. They said, "Yes, and we've assigned her to you." At that moment, I started to cry for the first time.

At 6:30 p.m., they started the Pitosin to begin contractions. At this time Casey's parents came back to see us. All I could say to them was what God had impressed upon my heart in the early morning of November 6 when I couldn't sleep: "God is still faithful." Apparently, that was difficult to hear.

When Charles and Cathy came to the room, Charles talked about what Jairus must have been thinking as they walked back to his house having heard that his daughter was dead. Yet Jesus said to him, "Only believe." We kept believing. (Luke 8:50).

My parents came to the delivery room. Marianne stayed in the room with us during everything Charles said, so it was good to have her hearing what we were believing for.

Other friends came and prayed great faith in that room. They mentioned how Jesus said to Martha before he raised Lazarus from the dead, "Only believe." We kept believing (John 11:40).

At that point, I asked Marianne if I could speak to Dr. Watson. I told her I was okay sounding like a lunatic, believing that God was going to work a miracle tonight. Dr. Watson said she too was a Christian and shared some of her beliefs. She said she cast no judgment on me.

I also asked Marianne if she would monitor the baby, so two or three times she placed the heart monitor on my belly and listened for a heartbeat.

As the contractions continued to get more intense, I asked that Casey come back into the room. I'm so glad I did because things progressed rather quickly. Right as Marianne walked out of the room, a contraction made the baby crown. I yelled, "She's coming out! Marianne! Marianne!" All of a sudden, the room filled with medical staff. Marianne held the baby's head when Dr. Watson came in. They moved me into position and with one or two good pushes, Selah Ann Cleveland was born at 11:26 p.m. I kept waiting and expecting her to amaze us all and cry...but she never did.

Marianne cleaned up Selah (pronounced SAY-luh) and brought her to me. Casey had already seen her and said she was beautiful. And he was right. She was absolutely beautiful! I held her and admired every part of Selah: her long fingers and toes, with fingernails that looked like they had been painted, her beautiful face and adorable nose. I even tried to look at the color of her eyes. She had very little hair, and it was covered in vernix, as was the rest of her body. Quite a lot of fluid had collected at the top of her head, so the top and back part of her head was full of it. The plates in her head were overlapped and moving a bit.

Beautiful Selah Ann was born weighing 9 pounds 9 ounces, and she was born on the sonogram due date— November 9. Since my original calculations put her being due on October 19, we had eagerly been anticipating her arrival for three weeks. I asked Marianne if she thought Selah was three weeks late or right on time. She seemed to think that with the amount of vernix on her and the amount of amniotic fluid in me that she was not late, since the later one goes, the less vernix and amniotic fluid there would be. This still left us with no answers as to what happened to her while in my womb. She was a perfect, beautiful baby…just without a heartbeat.

Several of us had the privilege of holding Selah, all of us with tears flowing down our cheeks. Our other midwife, Melissa, was working in the ER that night, so when she had a break, she came up. Her words were, "She's exactly where you said she was when we talked this morning."

And I asked, "Where did I say she was?"

"In the Lord's hands."

And I know she is, and of course, I receive great comfort knowing she is there, but missing her certainly is tough. As my sister-in-law Wendy said, "You love to be with those you love," and I love Selah. I long to be with her one day in the fullness of life.

A group of us gathered around our precious little one as I held her body, and Charles prayed for life to be restored, even though he only had a "mustard seed" of faith (Matthew 17:20). My mom then led us in singing "Jesus Loves Me." My sweet brother Doug was with us offering his love and support into the early hours of the morning.

Around 2:00 a.m., a photographer from an organization called Now I Lay Me Down To Sleep arrived to take pictures. I am so glad we had him take pictures, although some are very difficult to look at. We had to wake up Casey for the photos. During the photo shoot, he reached his emotional limit. He became angry at the whole situation and left the room for a while.

When the photographer was done, I wasn't exactly sure what to do. I knew we had been waiting up for the photographer to get here, and I knew I at least had that much time with my baby. Now that he was done, I knew my moments with her body were coming to an end. I wanted some time alone with her.

I held Selah in the wooden rocking chair, because that's what mommies do with their babies—they rock them. I prayed for God to show me what to do in these moments. I talked to Selah, quoted some Scriptures, and sang to her. I remember singing "My sweet, sweet girl," which is a silly song I sing to our boys ("My sweet, sweet boy"), and I tickle them on the high, off-pitch "sweet, sweet" part of the song. So I did the same for Selah— singing and tickling.

I had about fifteen minutes alone with her body before Casey came back in. We then had time together with Selah. The silence was broken when Casey said, "I just have to do this," and he started praying. We spoke to her spirit to come back into her body. I prayed that the

Holy Spirit inside of me would breathe life into her body, and then my mouth breathed into her mouth several times. When we were done praying, Casey simply said to me, "Thank you."

When we were all done, I placed her body back on the exam table, and I remember thinking as I cried, "I'm supposed to be laying you in your bed, not on this hard table."

We started to pack up our stuff to move to the Palliative Care floor. We left her on that table as I was wheeled out of the delivery room. That's when I remembered to sign and say "I love you," as I would do each night with our boys. It wasn't until I was being wheeled down the hallway by Marianne that I remembered I had not given Selah the blessing that I speak over my children every night at bedtime. At that moment, I said the blessing to her quietly as I rolled down the hallway.

By this point it was 4:00 a.m., so we had spent four-and-a-half hours with our beautiful baby. And, although we could have spent as much time as we wanted—no one rushed us in any way—her body had continued to deteriorate in the few hours we had with her.

After getting ready for bed, I called my friend Angela, since she told Cathy I could call anytime. It was good to talk to Ang and start to process all that had gone on in the hours prior. Her love and support across the miles have been invaluable.

It was around 5:00 a.m. when I went to bed, and Dr. Watson came in to check on me at 6:15 a.m. So I got about an hour of sleep.

It wasn't long before nurses, breakfast, and visitors started arriving. I called my MOPS (Mothers of Preschoolers) group since they were meeting that morning. They were already informed, and when it was announced that morning, I found out many of the other moms were in tears hearing of our loss.

My precious family circled around my hospital bed as we started to plan the Celebration of Life service for Selah.

By the time I was discharged at 3:00 p.m., we had Gentry Morrison set up to take care of funeral arrangements, and First Presbyterian Church was opening wide their doors to us to use whatever was needed for the service.

As Casey wheeled me down the hall toward the car, I shed many tears. Instead of a baby in my lap, I cradled a box of tissues. The nurses all stood and showed respect and sadness as I rode by.

I remembered when I rode out of the hospital holding Isaac in my arms thinking then that not all mommas get to take a baby home with them when they leave the hospital. Of course, I never dreamt that would be me only two and a half years later.

Casey took me straight to his parents' house where Solomon and Isaac had been since the day before. When Casey's mom dropped Solomon off at school that morning, she told the preschool director what had happened. When she picked him up only three hours later, the amazing people at the preschool had many bags of groceries for us, as well as several toys for the boys.

When Casey and I took Solomon and Isaac home, we all sat them on the couch and talked about their baby sister Selah. We explained to them that she is already in heaven with Jesus. At first, Solomon said, "No, she's in mommy's tummy."

I said, "It still looks like she's in mommy's tummy, but she's not; she's with Jesus."

Casey prayed with all of us, then showed Solomon a picture of her from our camera. Solomon noticed the skin around her eyes was red and asked, "Is she crying?"

At that moment, Casey and I started to cry and said, "No—she never cried." And of course, that's all we wanted her to do—was cry.

I explained to the boys that there would be crying around here, and that's okay. I explained that we wanted to bring Selah home with us, but we didn't get to and that makes us very sad. I said, "She'll never lie in her bed or wear her clothes, and we wanted her to do all that and so much more." I also explained that people would be coming by and things would be a little different for a while.

I'm not sure what all these little two- and four-year-old minds understood, but I'm certain these boys have a greater understanding of and appreciation for heaven since their sister Selah is there.

We ate dinner that had been so graciously provided for us and got ready for bed. I calculated that I was up for thirty-six hours with only sleeping one hour. I know the Lord is my strength.

In the days, weeks, and months ahead tears would flow—sometimes unexpectedly, sometimes uncontrollably. In reality, I felt like a chunk of my heart had been ripped from my chest. I knew I needed time to heal from this deep inner pain. And somehow I knew my heart would heal over time in the comforting arms of Jesus.

Tony's Studio of Photography

Beth Carter Photography

QUIET STRENGTH WHILE MY HEART HEALS

~ GOD, WHO ARE YOU?

My amazing sister Cathy took off work the rest of the week to be with me and to help us make arrangements for the Celebration of Life Service for Selah. Two days after Selah's birth, milk came in, which added to the difficulty of sleeping. I used cabbage leaves and ice packs to help ease the discomfort.

On Thursday, Cathy came over to help out again. She, my mom, and I went shopping for clothes for the service. After we visited a friend who contributed to my wardrobe, God provided the most perfect beautiful pink top and jewelry for the occasion. We also purchased shoes needed for the boys to dress up.

Cathy picked up the portrait of Selah, Casey, and me from the photographer. What a gorgeous picture of her—certainly a treasure for this hurting momma. This all felt so surreal. I felt like I was supposed to be happy about having a beautiful photo of my daughter, but I wanted more than a photo...I wanted my daughter with me!

Nonetheless, preparations were all coming together nicely for the next day's celebration service, and Casey's parents came over for dinner and to help with final plans.

Friday, November 13 was the day to join with family and friends to celebrate Selah. I woke up early to spend time with the Lord. It was a sweet time of prayer and personal worship for me. I worshiped with Hillsong's "Desert Song" which sings of the worth of our God. In every changing season of life, I can rejoice and worship because our God is unchanging.

I cried before the Lord and worshiped in the middle of my hurt and pain.

Still full of my milk, I had put cabbage leaves under my pajamas that morning. Casey and I had a good laugh when I got undressed for my shower and all I was wearing were these leaves. Casey mentioned it was like the Garden of Eden all over again.

As the four of us left the house to go to the Celebration of Life, we gave thanks to God for an absolutely beautiful day. It was a little cool and very sunny—hardly a cloud in the sky. It was a perfect day to celebrate our daughter.

We pulled into the parking lot of First Presbyterian Church at 9:30 a.m. and the visitation started at 10:00, with the service starting at 11:00 a.m. I was expecting more of an emotional meltdown when I saw Selah's casket, but I held together pretty well. It was a beautiful casket covered with pale pink material.

Solomon asked where Selah was, so I explained to him that her body was in the casket—the pink box—and that Selah herself is with Jesus in heaven.

I hugged a lot of necks and shed many tears during the visitation hour. Certain people brought additional tears—especially those people I had spent time with on Thursday, Friday, or Saturday, which were possibly Selah's final days. My guess is that Selah entered the arms of her Creator on Friday or Saturday morning.

I cried especially hard when I hugged my niece Tiffany because we had swapped kids' clothes. I gave her boy stuff that our boys had outgrown, and she gave me girl clothes for Selah to wear. I told Tiffany I knew it would be hard to walk into Selah's closet because it was pink and yellow and very cheery. There were so many clothes, blankets, towels, hair bands—the list goes on—that she will never use, and it was so difficult to fathom that right now.

I later found out that one of our family members had been praying and fasting for us and Selah. She arrived at FPC extra early and spent time in the backseat of the hearse by Selah's casket. Prayer and Scripture were read aloud. She was most confident Selah would cry out.

We are a family of great faith, expectant of God to do the impossible. And even though He didn't raise up Selah and heal her as we prayed, we still believe God is good and faithful.

We greeted people right up until 11:00 a.m. The Celebration for Selah service started with our dear friend Kate Lake reading Scripture from Psalm 139. Jessie and Ian Goodman led us in three worship songs. It was so beautiful and worshipful.

"Forever" by Chris Tomlin was chosen because our God is forever faithful. Plus, on the morning of Selah's birth, I had walked around our neighborhood and listened to and worshiped with the song "Forever." Either Isaac or I had changed the setting on my iPod because it kept repeating the same song. Finally, the third time "Forever" started to play again, I changed it.

"My Hope" by Darlene Zschech was chosen because throughout the delivery and hospital stay, the Experience CommUNITY song list was playing on Casey's computer. This was the song that stood out the most to me from that list, once again speaking of the faithfulness of our God.

"Jesus Messiah" by Chris Tomlin was chosen mainly because the bridge sings of our hope which is in the Lord. It's a beautiful song of declaration and praise.

As these songs were being so beautifully led, Casey and I both lifted up our arms in praise and surrender to the plan of our good Daddy God. Even with the wound of our hurting hearts so raw and exposed, we chose to sing these songs of praise, knowing our God truly is faithful and good.

Next, my parents read Scriptures concerning God being our Sustainer of life.

Charles gave the most beautiful message about Selah's life. One might wonder how, at a funeral for a stillborn baby, the preacher can talk about the child's life, but Charles did and he did a most wonderful job. He talked about the things Selah would have experienced in the nine months she was in my womb. First of all, she experienced hours of praise and worship—Sunday mornings and nights at Life Church, three Experience CommUNITYs, worship times with her mommy and daddy, rehearsals, and more. In fact, as we worshiped our faithful God at her service, I was thinking Selah would be familiar with all three of these songs and many others, too. I bet she has a beautiful singing voice—I can't wait to hear it!

Charles talked about how Selah would have experienced times of teaching, studying, and debating God's Word with others who were also hungry for it.

Selah also experienced hours of hearing her brother Solomon talk about dinosaurs and even roar like the T-Rex. She would have heard her brother Isaac say,

"Baby in tummy" as he would pat my belly.

Charles added some humor by saying that Selah would have also heard her daddy snoring. Anyone who has heard Casey snore would agree it is an undeniably loud sound!

Charles's message was really about life and God as the Creator and Sustainer of life. He also mentioned that his answer to the "Why?" question is "I don't know."

Then Jessie and Ian sang and played a song she wrote: "I Will Hide." This song has ministered to both Casey and me. In fact, just a week or so earlier I had been listening to Jessie's CD and that song stood out to me, albeit in different circumstances, of course.

"I WILL HIDE"

I will hide in the secret place.
My soul finds rest in God alone.
I will abide in the shadow of Your wings
Where I am safe.
My soul will cling to You.
Where does my help come from?
It comes from You,
The Maker of heaven, Maker of earth,
So I will hide.
You are my strength.
You are my shield.
You are my song.
You are the reason I am living.
© Jessie Goodman, 2006

Casey's parents finished with a Scripture reading from John 14. Gary was very bold in his reading, and I later found out he was working out his anger while fighting back his tears.

As he was finishing, Charles and I communicated about what was going to happen next. He told me a couple days before that he would do his best to communicate what Casey and I wanted said, but if he missed something, he would have a handheld mic available for us to say something. It was not on the program—just if we wanted to.

For the past few days, I had been trying to figure out how to bring closure to the fact that I had not given Selah her blessing on that first night. I was concerned about asking the funeral staff to open the casket for me because I wasn't sure what her body would look like after several days and I wanted to remember her the way she was when she was born. I thought of giving Selah her blessing either publicly or privately at the gravesite. It seemed like that might be a little awkward or maybe seem a bit thrown together. So when Charles mentioned a mic would be available, I considered that as a possibility. Even the morning of the service, I wasn't sure how the Lord would direct me concerning this, but I prayed He would.

When I mentioned to Casey that a mic would be available and I might share the blessing, he seemed a bit surprised, simply because the blessing is so personal and I would be sharing it in a public setting.

Well, in a public setting I did it. There were probably three or four hundred people there, and I stood up, took the mic, and walked over to the portrait of Selah, Casey, and me. Then Casey joined me.

I first thanked everyone for coming and for all their support. Then I said something like, "Every night growing up, my mom would speak a blessing over me. I have passed that legacy on to my children. Every night, I speak this blessing over our boys and every night when I would remember, I would speak it over Selah in my womb as I lay in bed. So, if you don't mind, I would like to speak it to her one last time—well, I'm sure it won't be the last. And if you can picture her in heaven with the Lord, these words are even more powerful." Then I turned toward her picture and said, "Selah, the Lord bless you and keep you." I started to cry as I thought of the Lord "keeping" her in His care in heaven. "The Lord make His face shine on you and be gracious to you. The Lord turn His face toward you and give you peace...and a good night's sleep" (from Numbers 6:24-26). Then I leaned down to her picture and gave her a kiss—only I was kissing glass instead of kissing her beautiful face.

Casey and I sat down and then I think Charles led us all in a prayer. Then we proceeded down the aisle toward the back of the sanctuary and into the cars to go to the gravesite.

Casey and I rode in the vehicle together behind

the car that carried her body. We reflected on the most beautiful service. I watched cars stop all the way down Bartow Road as they showed respect to us and our tragic loss.

I started to cry again as we drove into the Oak Hill Burial Park. It then hit me that we would have a gravesite to keep up and to visit. Things were so different than we had planned.

The graveside service was very short and sweet. Solomon sat with us on the front row while Casey's sister Rhea attended to Isaac. Charles spoke a few words and prayed, then each of us placed a tiny pink rose on Selah's casket.

We were escorted back to FPC with Charles and the funeral director in the front seats. We talked about the service together, and Charles said there was not a dry eye in the place once I turned to speak the blessing over Selah. In fact, he said from his perspective facing the people, we could have just counted "3-2-1" and watched the faces crinkle up and tears fall down. I looked through the guest book and noticed who had come to the service and visitation.

When we arrived at FPC, a good friend, Yvonne Hancock, and other Christian Women's Connection ladies had prepared a lovely lunch for us all.

When it was time for dessert, I announced that we had explained to the boys that we were having a combination of a church service and a birthday party for Selah.

Solomon asked if there would be a cake! So we had a cake that said "We Celebrate You, Selah" and we sang "Happy Birthday."

We spent time with family and friends, then Casey, Solomon, Isaac, and I, at Charles's direction, headed off to Orlando for the night. The boys fell asleep in the car while I opened cards. Everyone was so generous and supportive. When we got to Orlando, Casey stopped to get us some coffee at Starbucks. While he was in there, I opened cards and gifts that amounted to over $800—just in those few minutes! I told Casey he could go to Starbucks a lot more if we had that type of return every time!

We arrived at Quality Inn and Suites, and it was a nice place for such a reasonable rate. It had two separate bedrooms and two bathrooms, plus a sitting area and kitchenette. It was a short stay—only one night—but it was very nice.

Solomon was very excited about our evening plans—we had reservations at 6:45 p.m. to T-Rex Cafe, which was located at the then-called Disney Marketplace. We arrived early and allowed the boys to build a T-Rex at Build-A-Dino® store. Solomon named his Don (from "Ice Age 3: Dawn of the Dinosaurs," which he called the movie "Don the Dinosaur.") Solomon named Isaac's T-Rex John. Solomon enjoyed the store and sights at the restaurant while Isaac entertained himself for forty-five minutes going back and forth under the cloth ropes that direct the lines as people stand in them.

As one of the young ladies stuffed the boys' dinosaurs, she asked when my baby was due. I told her I had just given birth to a stillborn baby girl on Monday. Of course, it caught her by surprise—that was not the response she was expecting. In her shocked state, she said something to the effect, "Well, maybe you're just supposed to be a mom of boys."

Dinner was fun and loud. At various times the lights would change and the dinosaurs would "come to life." What a fun distraction from the events of the week!

On Saturday, we woke up and ate breakfast downstairs. We walked around Disney's Marketplace and Westside, and we said goodbye to all the dinosaurs at T-Rex Cafe before leaving.

We ate lunch at Uno's Pizzeria. Since we were stopping in Auburndale on our way home to go to Jeremy Harper and Joanna's wedding, I changed clothes in the bathroom of the restaurant. I remember in those few moments alone thinking about how we were leaving our mini-vacation to go back to life to this new normal. Tears started to flow again as I thought about it. I certainly didn't feel ready for this "new normal"...nor did I want it.

That evening, Casey, Stanley George, and Grant Ewert went to Tampa to lead worship and Gerry Hubbs came and spent the evening with me and the boys, so I wouldn't have to be alone yet. My mom brought flowers over from the Celebration service, as well as more food. Vicki Crews came and picked up laundry for us.

Gerry and I got to talk, and I shared with her some things about the past few days that I hadn't told anyone yet. We cried and my heart started to heal.

When Casey was in Tampa, he talked with Kay and Linda Faith. They had questioned the Lord about the events of the past week and even asked about clarifying the prophecies regarding our baby. They sensed the Lord saying something about how our ministry will begin to blossom now. Even Abraham didn't have to sacrifice his son, yet we had given up our daughter. The message was "God's love is mysterious."

*   *   *   *   *   *   *   *

On Sunday, all four of us made it to Life Church. I opted not to lead worship, but Casey really wanted to. It was a beautiful time of worship. Charles was so good to let me share with the people there. I talked about the events of the week and how God is so faithful, even though our circumstances are so unpredictable and painful. I encouraged the people to make this place (church) a safe place for us, to ask how we're doing, and not to feel awkward around us. And I cried as I said, "If you make it to heaven before I do, tell Selah how much I love her."

Mandy Crews brought six-week-old Baby Jonah to the church service for the first time. I was surprised how genuinely excited I was to meet him, being that he was only six weeks older than Selah.

That evening, Casey and I went to the cemetery—affectionately known as "Selah's Garden"—for the first time. We talked, cried, read Scripture, listened, and sang. Selah's grave is right beside her Great-Grammie, who passed in 1997. Of course, the dirt was still fresh from when they laid her casket in there. We brought Selah's portrait with us. It was a moving time.

As we turned to get in the car, we noticed what an absolutely beautiful pink sunset God had painted for us. It made me think Selah may have somehow contributed to the beauty of it.

Dinner arrived when we got home: Crispers brought by Kate Lake. We invited her to stick around. While we ate, Vicki arrived with more clean laundry. The four of us talked for a while. That's when I found out that, on Saturday, November 7, God had been individually preparing Kate, Vicki, and Lenore Holt for what was coming. On Saturday, Kate had a passing thought that the baby's heart had stopped. She prayed against it and didn't want to confess it. When she saw me that Sunday, she was purposeful about asking how the baby and I were doing. She was reassured by my answer that all was well. Vicki had been in St. Pete at her condo, and she had a feeling something was wrong. Her mind kept going to Casey and me and Selah, so she prayed for us. Lenore also had a feeling something was not right.

Monday, November 16 marked a week since Selah was born. My mom came over in the afternoon to be with us. We talked through the events of last Monday and what was happening at each particular hour. It was so good to have her there.

I was able to stay up and journal until 11:30 p.m. I sat on the couch downstairs in our home with Selah's portrait propped up on a chair. I had a cute, white, fluffy, plush toy bunny that Cathy had given to Selah. As 11:26 p.m. came around, I picked up the bunny and held it as if I was holding Selah. I had done that with both the boys—on their one-week birthday, I held and kissed and loved on them at the time they were born. This time, I hugged, kissed, and cried on what is now affectionately known as Selah Bunny. Oh how I miss her so much!

The next day, when the boys were down for their afternoon naps, I felt the Lord wooing me into Selah's closet. I spent some time there and cried exceptionally hard for the first time. I picked up different outfits and imagined her wearing them. Although it was very difficult, it was also a time of healing.

From November 26 through December 4, 2009, a precious family in the Lakeland area generously offered their gorgeous beach home to us, so we headed down to Anna Maria Island on Thanksgiving night. A policeman stopped Casey for speeding in the island's 25 mph zone, but he didn't give us a ticket since we were together as a family and it was Thanksgiving…thank You, Lord!

We enjoyed beautiful sunsets almost every night. On Saturday, my thirty-sixth birthday, we had about thirty people come over to celebrate my and Casey's birthdays. It was fun being with family and friends. Casey and his parents gave me a lovely ring with a pink stone and diamonds, and inside it is engraved "Selah Num. 6:24-26." It's my Selah ring and I love it!

We had a great week on the island. The boys were with us until Wednesday when we headed back to Lakeland for the day. Angela, now living in her home-state of Wisconsin, was in town so we got together for lunch.

My brief visit with Angela was interrupted by a gentleman arriving at our house with news of the early morning activities. His announcement informed us that our dream home was sold at the foreclosure auction that morning. This was certainly difficult to hear, but to be honest, after the loss of a child, the loss of our home seemed so minuscule.

Casey and I returned to the island alone for a couple more days. We got up one morning to see the sunrise but it was too cloudy—a little disappointing. But after breakfast, we were back in bed for our nap at 8:30 a.m.

I started listening to Steven Curtiss Chapman's album "Beauty Will Rise," written after the death of their daughter Maria. Oh how those songs have brought healing to my soul!

The night before Casey's birthday, the two of us enjoyed a dinner out on the island. Then we came home so we could take the boys to Disney's Hollywood Studios on Casey's birthday. We enjoyed their Christmas lights and a fun, cool day.

I remember one night after the boys went to bed, Casey was gone, and I was washing dishes while listening to the "Beauty Will Rise" album. I started to weep, and Casey came home. He hugged me and held me as I sobbed uncontrollably. The crazy thing is that Solomon came down the wooden stairs and climbed onto a kitchen chair. Neither one of us heard him. I only felt him grab me and hug me. Solomon has always been so tender toward my tears. He always tries to gently cheer me up, and he usually does a good job of it. As I watch Solomon interact with other babies, I know he would have been a great big brother to Selah . . .we'll just have to wait....

*　　*　　*　　*　　*　　*　　*　　*

The first baby I held after holding Selah was Jonah Crews. I asked his grandma Vicki if Mandy would be okay if I held him. They invited Casey and me to come over to their home. It was the Tuesday night before Christmas: December 22. It wasn't as emotional as I thought it would be—maybe because there was just a bit of activity at the house—TV, baking cookies...lots of cookies. While holding Jonah, the hardest part was his crying and wanting his mommy, and I had no baby on earth wanting that from me. I miss my Selah.

I started babysitting Jonah when he was four months old. Since Jonah was only six weeks older than Selah, caring for him on a regular basis through his first year of life was helpful in the healing process.

Since day one, we've communicated to the boys that Selah is with Jesus. Although her body is laid in a grave, her spirit is very much alive in heaven, and our confidence of that truth comes from the Bible. For several years, I had been taking a personal spiritual retreat in January of each year. 2010 was no different—I needed a little getaway with Jesus. After loading up my books, Bibles, and worship DVDs, I headed to Vicki's condo on St. Pete beach for one night.

It was a sweet time away of refreshment. When I arrived home late on Saturday night, certainly past the boys' bedtime, I was greeted by my sweet Solomon who decided to get out of bed when he heard me come home. After a hug, he very sincerely and innocently asked, "Did you bring Selah back with you?"

In this precious child's mind, he concluded that since Selah was "with Jesus" and I was going on a personal retreat to spend time "with Jesus," I would be bringing her home with me. Oh the beauty of the mind of a child!

In this season of intense hurting and disappointment, I asked many questions of myself and of God. My friend Yvonne brought clarity to my question as to why this all hurt so much. After all, it's not like I really knew Selah or had any special memories with her—yet the pain was intense at times. Yvonne's insight was that for nine months we had been anticipating Selah's arrival. The visual Yvonne offered was her hand moving up, like going up a mountain. With each passing day, our anticipation grew. Then suddenly, like dropping off an unforeseen cliff, our anticipation for life with our daughter here on earth unexpectedly ended. Much pain accompanies such loss.

Another question that resounded in my mind was "God, who are You? I mean really…who are You?" After thirty-five years of life and walking with the Lord for the majority of that time, I had a certain idea of who God was. But now—now I really wanted to know the truth as to who this God was that I worshiped and adored. I know, especially this side of heaven, we will never know the complexity and completeness of the God we worship, but He did begin to reveal Himself and bring more clarity to my question.

I know many people who find themselves in similar situations as ours also find themselves angry at God, blaming Him for their loss and hurt. I believe the advice I was given on that is wise: it's okay to be angry at God—just don't stay there.

Yet when Casey and I considered the nature of God and knew Him to be loving, faithful, and good, we chose to embrace Him in our pain and found great comfort in His arms.

What does embracing God in the midst of your pain look like? For us, it varied depending on the moment. Several times I would curl up on the bend of the couch and cry…truly cry…sometimes wail. I imagined myself in the arms of Jesus, and I sensed in a real way the peace and comfort of the Holy Spirit. Since this would often happen in the evenings, it was then that I would be able to fall asleep.

Sometimes I would just long to go to that spot on the couch to be comforted. Early on, Yvonne reminded me that Jesus said the Holy Spirit is the Comforter (See John 14:26 AMPC). He certainly was that for me many times. And when I didn't know how to pray (which was often), I would pray in my prayer language.

Casey's embracing of God oftentimes came through music. In fact, only two weeks after Selah was born, he wrote a most beautiful song called "Still Worthy." The lyrics of the song point to the fact that our circumstances do not change the character of God. Before Selah was born, we worshiped God with our whole hearts because we knew Him to be good and faithful (as stated in previous chapters). Now, although our circumstances had changed, God had not changed. He is still good…He is still faithful…He is still worthy of our praise.

"STILL WORTHY"

From the valley I'll rise up,
I'll rise up 'cause You are my strength.
You said You never will leave me,
Never leave me at any length.
And even when the darkness falls,
It's in the moments, I recall

You're still worthy,
Still worthy.
You are worthy of my praise.
You're still worthy,
So worthy,
Faithful to Your Word always.

In my hurting I find You,
I feel You, Lover of my soul.
You said You would redeem all things,
Redeem all things the devil has stolen.

And I do not understand it all.
There's so many questions "why?"
But that doesn't change who You are
And what You've promised me,
So here is my worship for Your glory.
© Casey Cleveland, 2010

Thursday, December 17 was one of those days when I took a much-needed nap. When I woke up, the look on Casey's face radiated confusion and concern. He told me that while I was napping, a sheriff came to the door. He informed Casey that, because our dream house had been sold at the foreclosure auction, we had twenty-four hours to be out of our home. Of course, this news threw Casey for a loop. This very kind sheriff apparently had one of our CDs and recognized Casey as being a member of the band Cleveland Carter years ago. This Christian sheriff encouraged Casey in profound ways, and even made a point to tell Casey that, although we only had twenty-four hours, he was not working the weekend, so no one would be back to check on us for a few days.

This news gave Casey and me and our precious church family a little extra time to pack up the house and make a plan. For the immediate future, Casey's parents graciously opened their home up to the four of us, where we lived for the next two weeks, including Christmas.

As Casey drove around the area looking for rental homes, he noticed a modest home in an area we preferred, yet the sign read "For Sale By Owner." Since our credit was shot at this point, we knew we could not buy a home, so Casey passed by. Yet he felt the tug of the Holy Spirit to call the number on the sign.

As an act of obedience and trust, Casey called the number. At first the gentleman on the line was not willing to rent, yet in this one conversation, he already wanted Casey to live in his home. He gave Casey the code to get in the house. As he looked around at this lovely, recently remodeled home on a dead-end street, Casey knew this was the house for us.

As only God could do, the owners of the house decided to let us rent instead of buy. We developed a sweet relationship with these owners, and this house became a place of refreshment and healing.

On January 1, 2010, trucks and amazing friends and family arrived at our new home on moving day. All went smoothly as we started our new life in a new place.

The next day brought the news that the first baby born in Polk County in 2010 was named Selah. This news hit me hard, and I found myself in my new closet sobbing.

Casey and I continued to be worship leaders at Life Church Lakeland, where my brother-in-law Charles Asbridge and my sister Cathy were the pastors. Being in the presence of the Lord was healing, but with it came other emotions. Whenever Mandy was there with Baby Jonah, I realized I was fine up there leading worship when he was in his car seat, sitting beside her. But as soon as Mandy was holding Jonah in her arms, the tears would start to flow, even from the platform.

A couple of other stinging-heart moments happened at MOPS (Mothers of Preschoolers). I loved being a part of our MOPS group. In fact, my table leader was one of the first people I called while I was still in the hospital after Selah was born. At first I didn't think I could go back to our weekly MOPS meetings right away. I didn't think I could handle all the mamas and their little ones. But on the other hand, I thought it would be healthy to surround myself with other mamas who loved me and would support me through this difficult season. In fact, I remember Casey's delightful surprise when I told him I was going back to MOPS the next week after Selah's birth.

One week, I sat in our MOPS meeting where over eighty moms met. Behind me, I could hear the sounds of a little baby sucking milk. That had always been such a delightful sound, but this time, it was piercing to my heart, knowing a little baby was enjoying his mama's milk while I never had that with Selah. The sting lessened a bit when I turned around to notice this baby was not drinking his mama's milk, but milk from a bottle because this precious little one had recently been adopted, and I knew this mama had had her own challenges with infertility.

In late November 2009, the MOPS leaders recognized all the moms who had had babies that semester by giving each of them a MOPS burp cloth. I wasn't sure if they would give one to me; after all, I gave birth to a baby but certainly had no reason for a burp cloth. And let's admit it, people don't know how to respond to mamas of stillborn babies…it's a mysterious life.

If I'm honest, I wanted them to recognize Selah's life, but at the same time, I didn't want to be recognized because my situation was very much a downer compared to all the joy on display by the other moms of newborns.

When the little ceremony had concluded, Selah's birth was not recognized, and I found myself in tears. These tears were different from the tears that I would normally cry at the MOPS meetings. But before I left, Tiffany Belbin said she felt God told her to give her burp cloth to me. I was very grateful. Now I had tears of joy because I knew God had remembered me and used a precious friend to share His love—and hers—with me. (I also made sure Tiffany received another burp cloth for her kindness shown to me.)

At our new house, Casey hung a shelf with a rod. The shelf holds Selah's portrait, as well as other mementos related to Selah. On the rod hangs the MOPS burp cloth, as well as the blanket we wrapped her in, which still has some of her blood on it, and the First United Methodist Church prayer quilt—every knot symbolic of a prayer for us. FPC gave us a pink prayer shawl, and necklaces with Selah's picture on it were given to us by Dawn McDonald and Tiffany and Scott Williams.

On May 11, 2010, I had the privilege of sharing our journey for the first time publicly to the MOPS group. Sharing our story and what God had sustained us through up to that point was another step in our healing.

*   *   *   *   *   *   *   *

Not long after Selah's birth, I came to the conclusion that since I could not know Selah here, I wanted to find out all I could about where Selah is. Years prior, I had decided to make the Bible, God's Word, the roadmap of my life. There's a story in the Bible regarding the death of King David's seven-day-old son. In his deep sorrow, David said, "I will go to him, but he will not return to me" (II Samuel 12:23).

With that confidence—and other Biblical truths—I am more than confident that Selah is in heaven, and because of my faith in Jesus Christ, God's Son, as my Savior, I believe I will join Selah in heaven when my days on earth are complete.

Since I didn't have the privilege of knowing Selah here on earth, I started reading several books about heaven and finding out as much as I could about where she is.

In fact, I did the Beth Moore study on Revelation, and I remember one day reading about the Battle of Armageddon and the Marriage Supper of the Lamb and just crying. I think most of it was due to the fact that no matter what happens—death, rapture, or whatever—by the time of these prophetic events, Selah and I will be together...forever! I really look forward to that day!

Through the Beth Moore study, Tee, Casey's mom, confirmed her decision to receive Jesus as her Savior. For years, she had questions about her salvation because she never had a "lightning bolt" experience. I prayed, "Lord, whatever it takes…." On this one night particularly, the study was especially powerful, so I asked Tee if I could share the information with her. In front of the fireplace at our new home, still with lots of questions in her mind, Tee prayed to receive Christ (for sure) on March 4, 2010.

When I called her the next morning, Tee admitted to the fact that she felt different that day. She was more joyful and certainly confident in her decision to accept Jesus as her Savior—the best decision ever! In fact, she was the one who mentioned her spiritual birthday being on March 4th or "march forth."

Although the hurt of the death of our daughter is extremely painful, any time something good comes from our loss, it brings purpose to our pain. Tee's decision to trust Christ, even in the midst of her own pain and loss, was one of those huge blessings that has come through our intense hurt, which gives purpose to the pain.

Selah's four-month birthday was a tearful day. It was a Tuesday, so I stopped by Selah's Garden before going to MOPS, where I had nursery duty that day. I was with little ones who were slightly older than Selah, which I suppose made it a little easier.

Then I asked to hold a four-month-old little girl whose name was Kaitlyn. She must have been tiny when she was born because she was just a little thing!

After MOPS, I stopped at the birthing center's parking lot and cried and cried. Although Selah's four-month birthday was a hard day, I found the tears to be instrumental in the healing of my heart.

Isaac and I went to Selah's Garden on his third birthday. That was a hard day—deeply wanting Selah to be here to celebrate her brother. As we left the cemetery, a funeral procession drove down Bartow Road. I wasn't sure if it was appropriate for our side to pull off the road in respect, but I noticed a van pull over, so I did, too.

We were beside each other at the next light, so I asked the driver, "Have you been there?"

"Yes," she said.

"Me too."

She added, "God is going to get us through."

I agreed. And drove off and cried some more.

On Sunday, May 2, 2010, I took a pregnancy test, not because I thought I was pregnant, but because Casey and I were planning to fast for three days. If I wasn't going to be eating for a few days, I wanted to be sure I wasn't starving a little one inside me.

To my surprise, the pregnancy test was positive! At first I cried. I wasn't sure I was ready to be pregnant again. It hadn't even been six months since Selah's birth.

Was my body ready? Was I stable enough emotionally? I had lots of questions and fears to face.

It was the early hours of a Sunday morning. Casey wasn't awake yet, and I knew I would be seeing Cathy at the church service in just a few hours, so I called her first. As always, she offered hope and encouragement, helping me to overcome my fears.

The first sonogram appeared to show a little girl. I was thrilled that God was answering Cathy's prayer that God would give us another girl—thrilled at the thought of having a little girl wear all the cute pinks and yellows that had been ready for Selah.

Three weeks later, the level II ultrasound showed my healthy baby to be a boy!

Don't get me wrong—I love all my boys very much, but this announcement "reopened the wound in my heart," as Cathy put it. I've now been told twice I would have a girl to raise on this earth…still no girl.

I have always had a wonderful relationship with my mom and sister. I have such great memories of shopping outings together with the three of us. Since I enjoy manicures and pedicures, I imagined girly outings with my daughter(s). Not to mention prom dress shopping and wedding planning….

    *   *   *   *   *   *   *   *

Mother's Day was Selah's six-month birthday. I made sure Casey knew I could use a special day, but the night before, I got the idea he had good intentions but not great follow-through. I was mad. I even yelled loudly at the mantle with my fist as I gave Selah her blessing.

Each night, as I stand at her portrait on the mantle and speak the blessing from Numbers 6:24-26 over her, I imagine her being held by Jesus or a loved one. I literally see Jesus "turn His face toward you now." I believe, somehow, Selah is aware each night as I give her her blessing. So, this night, when I was so mad, I really didn't want her seeing me in that state—which made me madder! So I prayed God would wake Casey up so it would be a special day.

Casey must have said the same prayer, because at 4:00 a.m., he was wide awake! At that early hour, he went to Walmart. I was awakened at 5:56 a.m. by Solomon bringing me a rose. Then breakfast came to me in bed. After a while, Isaac brought me a rose. Practical gifts showed up—flip flops and a pink water bottle with all the kids' names written on it. However, the card only had the boys' names on it—not Selah's.

Please understand, six months into this journey, I was still trying to navigate how to keep Selah a part of our family, even though she was not physically here with us. Yet she is still a member of our family. She's still one of our children.

In the early days of this struggle, my mom mentioned a friend of ours who had a stillborn child. When asked how many children she had, she always included her stillborn child in that number. For a heart-hurting mom, this made sense to me as a simple way to keep Selah part of our family.

After opening my sweet gifts and card and eating a yummy breakfast in bed, we went to Lake Parker for our Mother's Day church service. Lenore gave me the gift she had given to each of our kids: the child's name and birthdate written beautifully and framed. I also held a little girl while we were at the park.

We came home and took a nap, and I reset the alarm to the exact time I thought God told me to. When the alarm went off, it was the first words of the song "Song for My Sons" by Sara Groves. Sara now has a girl, too. I felt like it was a God-moment.

After our naps, we went to Selah's Garden. We sent up three pink balloons. I wrote a love note to Selah on my balloon and let it go up to the sky.

Then Isaac and Solomon let theirs go. I watched Solomon's until it was swallowed by a cloud and at that moment, I sensed, "Got it!"—just as if it was in heaven being given to Selah to enjoy!

From there we went to Anna Maria Island for dinner at Oma's Pizza. We then enjoyed the beach and the most beautiful sunset I think I have ever seen! It was as if Selah and God painted it for me. At that moment, I was so glad we had made the trip to the beach.

On the ride home, Solomon wanted to hear the Bible story of Jonathan's Balloons that Pam Mutz wrote and I had read earlier that day. Jonathan's Balloons was written in memory of her little boy Jonathan who drowned in the bathtub many years prior. Pam, in all her wisdom and guidance, knew how to love me well in my grief because she had experienced similar grief years before.

It wasn't until we got home and I looked up at Selah's picture that I noticed a rose and a card "from Selah." The card was just perfect and the last one on the store shelf—it was saved just for us. It read:

Butterfly kisses for my Special Mommy—
Can't say how much I love you
And, Mommy, here is why—
I'd have so many reasons
They'd reach right up to the sky!

Happy Mother's Day
XOXO
-Selah Ann
2010

Both of my moms were understanding and allowed me to have "my time" on Mother's Day. So I had planned a special breakfast with both my mom and mother-in-law the next morning.

Casey and I fixed them a delicious breakfast at our home. After breakfast, I gave them each a Mother's Day card, signed by each of us, including Baby #4 on the way! That's right…that's how both families were informed about our growing family.

Just like us, I'm sure both moms were excited yet apprehensive as we faced another pregnancy so soon after Selah's birth.

Tony's Studio of Photography

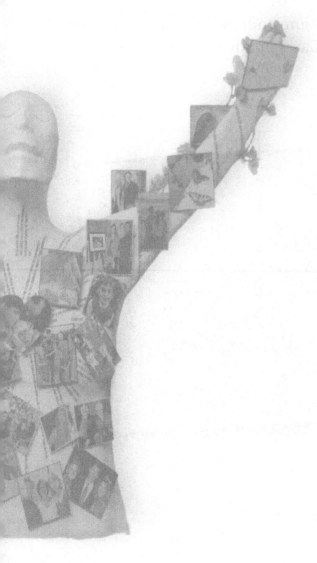

Quiet Strength Through Disappointment

~ My Heart Hurts Again

In the fall of 2010, I started homeschooling Solomon using the Classical Conversations model. This allowed me to take on a part-time position in the music department at Lakeland Christian School from which I graduated in 1992. Several of my nieces and nephews attended LCS, and my "Seester" Cathy taught chemistry half days there.

I enjoyed working with such wonderful people, and best of all, Cathy and her bubbly self would come bouncing into the piano lab every now and then to bring a little more sunshine to us all.

Cathy was two years and two months older than me. Growing up, I followed in her footsteps in nearly every capacity. Several of my siblings took piano lessons, and being the youngest of six, I too was bound to take lessons. However, Cathy and I were the only two that stayed with piano for any length of time.

In fifth grade, Cathy started playing the flute, so when I entered fifth grade, guess what instrument I chose...that's right, the flute. We also took years of voice lessons and sang together many times.

Cathy was an awesome cheerleader at Evangel Christian School, which is the school we attended for most of our education. As soon as I was old enough, I too became a cheerleader. It was always the most fun when we could cheer Evangel's basketball team on to victory, especially since our brother Greg was the star player.

Also, I played softball because Cathy played softball.

Not only was Cathy gifted musically and athletically, best of all, she loved Jesus and was not ashamed to show it. As the younger sister, I observed her (and my mom) as she developed a regular Bible reading and prayer time. Cathy's life inspired me to fall in love with Jesus, to spend time with Him daily in prayer and Bible reading, and to live out my love for Jesus on a daily basis.

Cathy graduated from Evangel Christian School and then moved onto the campus of Florida Southern College. For my last three years of high school, I transferred to LCS, and after graduating, went to Florida

Southern as well.

As a freshman, it was useful having an older sister there to show me around and introduce me to people. When it came time to choose a sorority, I thought it was time to branch out and go my own path. However, I couldn't help but choose the same sorority Cathy had chosen three years before. The sisterhood of Kappa Delta became a sweet place for me, and Cathy was instrumental in that.

While at FSC, I pursued a Bachelor's degree in music education with emphasis on voice. Although Cathy's major was biology, she continued to play her flute in the concert band, which gave me reason to see her occasionally around the music department.

During her college years, she met her future hubby Charles Asbridge. But before marrying, Cathy's beauty, talent, and personality gave her great reason to pursue competing in pageants through the Miss America system. All three years Cathy competed, she made it to the Top Ten at Miss Florida. We were so proud of her!

As you may have guessed by now, although my time was very brief, I too pursued the pageant route, being inspired and motivated by my beloved Seester. I enjoyed sharing those experiences with her and being consulted by her whom I would consider one of the best.

Our lives drifted apart for a few years, not because we loved each other any less, but only because our lives were at different stages in the mid- and late-1990s. I was still in college and Cathy was now a newlywed. And then in 1998, Charles Burman Asbridge III ("Tripp") was born. Cathy was now a mom…and a great one at that!

When Tripp was eighteen months old, Cathy and Charles received some very unexpected news. After having a mole removed on her arm, simply because it kept getting caught on her bracelet, we discovered Cathy had melanoma.

Obviously, this diagnosis surprised us all, especially since Cathy was such a healthy twenty-eight-year-old. The mole was removed, her diet was changed, and as far as we knew, all was well.

In 2006, when Cathy was pregnant with their fourth child Christopher, we were faced with the reality of Cathy's second diagnosis of melanoma. I remember her performing a flute and guitar duet with Charles as they played the beautiful hymn "'Tis So Sweet to Trust in Jesus." And that's exactly what they did. They trusted Jesus through this difficult part of the journey.

Personally, I remember worshiping the Lord through a song titled "Blessed Be Your Name," which speaks of blessing and praising the name of the Lord when life is great and when life is difficult.

Although I'm fairly certain Cathy lived with the concern of melanoma, we had reason to believe her body was clear of this disease. That's why we were so shocked when in November 2010 Cathy was diagnosed with stage four melanoma.

When Cathy became sick, I first found out about it while I was working at LCS one day. I went by her classroom after school and Tripp informed me that she was home sick. Of course, we just thought she had a bad case of the flu or something.

But in the early hours of a November morning, we found ourselves in the disbelief of realizing the cancer had spread to her brain. Later we found out it was in various organs of her body.

Before being discharged from the hospital, Cathy started her ten-day radiation treatment on her brain to help shrink the tumor. Cathy's faith remained strong as we all prayed and believed for her complete miraculous healing.

It was extremely difficult to see her body and her mind deteriorate in those last five months of her life. Yet on March 29, 2011 at 12:05 p.m., Cathy took her last breath here on this earth and entered the glorious and peaceful presence of her Lord and Savior Jesus Christ.

Earlier that morning, the doctors informed us that her body's organs were shutting down, and they were not expecting her to survive much longer. Since Cathy was so loved by so many, the hospital room was full of family and close friends in her final hours here.

My mom recalls Cathy looking at each one of us as we stood around her hospital bed, as if to say goodbye to us all.

Starting at Psalm 145, I read aloud from my Amplified Bible. Psalms 145-150 are beautiful songs of praise, and as if on cue, when I completed reading the final hymn of praise, Cathy's heart stopped beating-...she had entered the presence of our Lord. Here's how I see it: Cathy saw the beautiful face of Jesus, and I believe His beauty literally took her breath away.

Obviously, we were not ready for her to leave us, so the doctors attempted resuscitation to no avail. I was still at a stage of great faith, believing that God could even raise Cathy from the dead. I asked the nurses to take the tubes and IVs out of her body and instructed Charles and Casey to remain in the room to pray for Cathy to be raised up. My prayers continued fervently in the waiting room, expecting God to do the miraculous.

After several minutes, Charles and Casey returned and the miracle we had prayed and believed for was not our reality. Cathy was completely healed, but in a different realm.

Now it was time for Charles to go tell their four young children that Mommy was with Jesus. As I understand it, Charles and his mom Wanda met in Julie Rice's office at LCS. The children were dismissed from their classroom and were told of their mommy's homegoing.

No doubt, tears were shed and a "new normal" needed to be discovered.

Once again, First Presbyterian Church, where Charles had served as youth pastor for over a decade, opened wide their arms to us and our family as we planned yet another Celebration of Life service.

At the 11:00 a.m. service on Friday, April 1, 2011, there was not another seat available in the 875-seat sanctuary at FPC, and probably not a dry eye either. It was standing room only and out the door with over a thousand people in attendance. In Cathy's thirty-nine years of life on this earth, she touched the lives of countless people by her life, love, and faith.

Cathy's bubbly personality brought joy to all around her. On numerous occasions when I entered a room of people where Cathy already was, she would come up to me, so excited to see me there, as if I were the most important person in the room. I always thought she made me feel that way because of our special connection as Seesters. But following her passing, I realized she had a unique way of making every single person who walked in the room feel like they were the most important person there. Everyone who knew Cathy loved her.

Not only did Cathy's personality draw people to her, but everyone admired her for her gorgeous "everlasting smile." In fact, in high school, Todd Christian used to call Cathy "Smiley" because there was always a smile on her face.

But let's be honest, Cathy had her struggles, too. She had bad days and disappointing moments, but for 99.9% of the time when you encountered Cathy, she was joyful and absolutely delightful.

After Cathy's passing, we had many questions and disappointments. We had prayed and truly believed—even beyond all logical belief—that Cathy would be miraculously healed. So why wasn't she? In fact, some members of the family began to ask such questions as, "Why pray?"

Here's my perspective, and I think it's Biblically based.

When we look back at the Garden of Eden, we have a beautiful picture, not only of a perfect creation, but also of the beautiful and perfect nature of God. The Garden of Eden is God's ideal for us all.

We have to remember that death was never part of God's original design, but when sin entered the world through Adam and Eve's disobedience, death became a reality to us all.

Fast-forward several millennia to 2011, when I'm asking myself the question, "Was this God's 'perfect will' for Cathy to die?" Based upon what I know of God's good character through the perfect world He originally created, I don't believe Cathy's death was what God really wanted either. Yet she died.

We know from Scripture that it is our enemy, the devil, who "comes only to steal and kill and destroy" (John 10:10).

Here's the good news…here's the hope:

Because we love God and are called according to His purpose (and the same is true of Cathy too), we have the confidence of knowing God is working all things together for good (Romans 8:28).

At some point before Cathy's passing, Casey and I started listening to teachings by a gentleman with an effective healing ministry. One day while listening, I remember the gentleman mentioning something to this effect: "What if you pray for twenty people to be healed and none of them are healed? Will you keep praying and believing for number twenty-one or will you give up at twenty, coming to your own conclusion that God doesn't heal anymore today?"

After hearing that, I knelt down at my prayer chair and begged God, "Please don't let Cathy be one of those twenty who doesn't get healed!"

Even so, her healing was not on this earth as we had prayed and believed. And although we miss her deeply, we rest in the assurance that God is working out good, even in our loss.

Philippians 1:6 encourages me: "And I am sure of this, that He who began a good work in you will bring it to completion at the day of Jesus Christ." (ESV)

I do see God doing a "good work" even in Cathy's passing. But in addition to the good work He's doing, this is what excites me most: "He...will bring it to completion at the day of Jesus Christ" (Philippians 1:6). That tells me the purpose of Cathy's life and her influence upon the world will continue, even until Jesus returns to get His bride. Now that's awesome!

Even death can't stop God from completing what He's started in us! Hallelujah—thank You, Jesus!

God's good work in Cathy will continue in the legacy of her precious children. They each love Jesus and are continuing the good work that Cathy sowed in each of them, even in their few years together.

I was reminded of the positive influence and the "good work" that the Lord continues to do through Cathy's life and witness when I received a message from one of the pageant organizations that Cathy was a part of back in the early 1990s.

The Miss Tampa organization contacted me because they were wanting to rename one of their awards to The Cathy Pike-Asbridge Spirit Award. The lady who contacted me apologized profusely that this award was not renamed years ago, and I reaffirmed her that it actually means more to me that five years after Cathy's passing, she is still remembered and still making an impact. ". . . He will bring it to completion at the day of Jesus Christ."

Two months before Cathy's passing, there was a

time of great rejoicing as new babies were being born. Babies…yes, plural.

In the previous chapter, I talked about my discovery that I was pregnant again only six months after Selah was born. Although I was excited, fear knocked on my door. Cathy walked this journey with me, encouraging me and helping me to overcome my fears.

Cathy was the first person I called to tell her I was pregnant. Cathy was the one who mourned with me most closely as I wrestled through not having another girl, as we were told after the first ultrasound.

On January 11, 2011, our precious little Daniel was born at 7:26 p.m. By this point, Cathy was too sick to join me in the delivery room as she had done for my previous three births.

What made this day doubly exciting was the fact that while I was being induced to give birth to Daniel, my brother Greg and his wife Mandy were in Connecticut giving birth to twins. Garrett and Elizabeth Pike were born only five hours before Daniel, also on the unique date written 1-11-11.

I have sweet memories of my mom sitting with me while we awaited Daniel's arrival. She was receiving calls and texts from Greg with the latest news on the twins' delivery.

I remember that day being full of grace and joy, even in the midst of all the sadness and uncertainty of

Cathy's cancer diagnosis. January 11 brought much-needed smiles to all of our faces as these three new babies represented perfect health and life.

At Cathy's Celebration of Life service, Casey and I sang "We Still Believe" by Kathryn Scott. Once again, regardless of our circumstances—the good, the bad, and the ugly—we still choose to believe in the goodness of our God.

Each year on Cathy's birthday we find unique ways to celebrate her life. On September 16, 2018—her forty-seventh birthday—I encouraged friends on Facebook to write a favorite memory of Cathy. Here is a sweet interaction between a few of us regarding Cathy and her amazing smile. (See more posts in Appendix II.)

> **Hannah R.** – I remember her running every lap of LCS's Boosterthon with Chris because he wouldn't let go of her hand. It was a million degrees and she had on nice clothes and she still looked perfectly put together and kept up with all those kids. I was in awe!
>
> **Cindy Cleveland** – Love this picture of Cathy and Christopher! Darise M. sent this picture to me recently, and apparently it was taken on Cathy's thirty-ninth birthday, September 16, 2010, only one month before she got sick.
>
> **Hannah R.** – YES!!! I'll never forget this. She ran laps around the field in extreme heat in sandals, for crying out loud! And she smiled and looked radiant the whole way. Every time Cathy went

by I told her she was putting us all to shame!

Cindy Cleveland – This photo embodies so much of Cathy, especially her smile and her love for her children while still loving on others, while exercising and carrying on for the cause of Christ. She's amazing!

Hannah R. – This has always been my favorite memory of her. What an unexpected treasure that it was recorded on camera!

Darise M. – Who could ever forget her beautiful smile. She always radiated happiness!

On March 29, 2019, I posted this message on a group chat of Kappa Delta Sisters:

Hey Sisters. Just wanted to share that it was eight years ago today that Cathy Pike Asbridge saw the beautiful face of Jesus. Please consider a sweet memory with her, or even how your life is touched by her still today. Also, please say a prayer for her kids and Charles and family. Thanks for being a true sisterhood and sticking with us through the good and difficult seasons of life.

Amy T. – Cathy somehow knew your spirits

needed lifted before you did. She was a *kindness ninja.*

Leslie H. – It's really hard to put into words how Cathy touched each of our lives. Her incredible spirit, her zest for life, her love for the Father and her beautiful family. She touched each of us with her amazing smile and her beautiful soul. We rest in the knowledge of Cathy welcoming others into Heaven the same way she welcomed us into KD and touched our lives forever…we will never forget.

Susan F. – Love both the Pike girls! Such great memories of our college days. Cindy, it was so sweet to be a witness to your triple sisterhood with Cathy (spiritual, biological, and KD sorority). Look forward to seeing Cathy again when we all get to our heavenly home. You know she'll have that beautiful smile for us. Much love to all of you!

QUIET STRENGTH IN FIGHTING

~ PRAYER WORKS, MY FRIENDS

When Daniel was only four weeks old, Casey and I started ministering with a church in Daytona Beach. After several months of traveling back and forth every weekend (two hours one way) and after much prayer, I announced to my parents, only two weeks after Cathy's passing, that Casey and I and the boys would be moving to Daytona Beach.

Although this was an exciting adventure and opportunity, leaving my family at this time of loss was difficult. Casey was still doing work in Lakeland even after we moved to the east coast, so now we were traveling back to Lakeland each Sunday after services. This meant we still had frequent opportunities to be with family and stay close and connected.

During this time, Casey and I only had one vehicle—a bright yellow Mazda Protege 5. The "5" was because the car had a fifth door, a hatchback. But it also only had five seats, which meant two car seats and a booster seat were squished together in the backseat on all of these road trips back and forth on Interstate 4.

Since we only had one car, most weekends we traveled together as a family, but I remember one Sunday Casey leaving to go to Lakeland while the three boys and I stayed in our home in Ormond Beach. Here I was, three little guys and me at home with no transportation for a couple days. Thankfully, we had a precious church family who was willing to help out as we needed it. All was well and we survived our days stuck at the house.

It seems God kept placing us in churches with a significant number of challenges and changes. Now that I think of it, maybe that's every church.

Midway through Casey's time as the worship leader at Word of Faith Family Church, the Daytona Beach congregation had to move locations, and it started another congregation in the Orlando area. Before completing our time at WOFFC, we started our Sundays at the service in Daytona Beach; after the worship set, we would leave to lead worship at the Orlando location. Then we would pack up the boys and drive to Lakeland to participate in worship at the evening service at Life Church in Lakeland. Sundays were full!

During our time on the east coast, we discovered that our family was continuing to grow. When we went for the ultrasound, I told the sonographer about our experience with Selah and also how we were told with my next pregnancy (Daniel) that I was having a girl. So I told her, "Do not tell me I'm having a girl unless you are absolutely sure!"

On the monitor on the wall, Casey and I and the boys could see what the sonographer was seeing on her screen. I remember thinking, "That looks like a boy-part." At that moment, she said, "Well, I'm not going to tell you you're having a girl!"

Four boys! Although I was super-excited to have a great report of a healthy baby, part of me truly wanted a girl to raise, so a little disappointment mixed with all the excitement...just to be honest.

I called my bestie in Daytona Beach, Susan Mac-Donald, to let her know the report from the ultrasound. She often spoke words of hope and encouragement, and this time was no different. Susan said, "Cindy, it's a high calling to raise four boys!"

Susan was right. God has called, empowered, and blessed Casey and me with the privilege of raising these four boys to be great leaders for the Kingdom of God. Wow, I am a blessed woman!

After a year of living in Ormond Beach, the Lord led us back to Lakeland. Casey's parents opened wide their hearts and their home to the five of us (plus one on the way) moving in.

This time our stay lasted five or six weeks before we found a beautiful home that had been recently remodeled. To make the home work for our purposes, we added a music studio to the back of the house. Because our financial situation was still very much on the rocks and our credit was shot, a family member purchased our home and we became the renters.

September 29, 2012 was moving day. September 30 was our due date. We weren't sure which was coming first—house or baby? House won.

On October 1, while busily unpacking boxes, I received a call from my midwife saying that the doctor who was planning to induce me in the hospital would like me to come to the hospital to be checked. We quickly made arrangements for the boys, and Casey and I headed over to the hospital.

The doctor decided everything looked good, and since I was there, he suggested that we just go ahead and start the induction. So that's what we did!

At 2:46 a.m., Josiah entered this world just as perfect as could be, weighing in as my second largest: 9 pounds 10 ounces.

By the time Josiah and I came home a couple days later, Casey and his mom had worked extra hard to make us all feel comfortable in our new abode, even hanging some pictures on the walls already!

New baby. New home. I felt like it was the start of a new chapter in our lives. And it was.

After several months, Casey took a worship-leading position at Shepherd's Community United Methodist Church in south Lakeland. He was also working as a marketing and technical director at a local dentist office. Charles and Casey continued their work together as a video production company.

Josiah was a delightful baby. Daniel was becoming a very curious and extremely active toddler.

I still homeschooled Solomon and Isaac using the Classical Conversations model. They excelled in learning their material. I was so proud of them when on April 8, 2014, Solomon and Isaac both became Memory Masters through the CC model for the third year in a row! This is a very high honor, and they worked extremely hard to accomplish this goal.

To celebrate, we invited their dad and grandparents to join us at PDQ for a delicious lunch. Casey and our friend (and sound guy) Randy were able to slip away from their very strenuous work at Shepherd's. Easter Sunday, the deadline to finish the new stage, sound, and lighting for the sanctuary quickly approached, and Casey, Randy, and their team were working long days to complete it before then.

After getting the four boys to bed that night, I stayed up to write a blog post about Solomon and Isaac reaching their Memory Master goal. This activity kept me up later than usual, which was good, because I was glad to still be awake when Casey arrived home at midnight.

He showed me pictures of their progress from the day at Shepherd's. We discussed the activities of the day and after showering, went to bed around 1:00 a.m.

At 4:30 in the morning, Casey sat up in bed and said, "No, God! No!" I think Casey knew at that point that whatever was happening was at the root a spiritual battle.

Casey then felt sick to his stomach, but couldn't seem to get out of bed to get to the bathroom. I got him the family barf bucket, but then he indicated he was hungry. Since he wasn't clearly communicating what he wanted, I got him some crackers and water.

I don't recall if he ate any of the crackers, but I do remember he did something very odd—he tried to drink his water while lying down. Of course, when the water spilled on his face and pillow, he became frustrated.

He also told me he needed to go "pee pee." Those with young children may understand that words like "pee pee" are frequently said around the house. Although it was common lingo when communicating with our boys, Casey made it clear that he never liked that particular term. So for him to be telling me at that hour that he had to go "pee pee" was quite humorous to me! I remember thinking how funny it would be when I tell him in the morning that he said he needed to go "pee pee" in the night.

Since I wasn't exactly sure what was going on, I decided to stay up and have my morning quiet time with the Lord on the floor beside our bed. I remember pulling up a song on my phone that was fairly new to us at the time. It spoke great truth to me in those moments. The lyrics of "Your Grace Finds Me" written by Matt Redman filled my heart and mind and ministered to me in ways I didn't know I needed at the time. Still today, I can't hear that song without it connecting me to God's grace to me in those moments.

About 5:30 a.m., I called Casey's mom Tee to tell her something was not quite right with Casey and wasn't sure if we might need to get him to the hospital. I told her I would keep her posted.

Since this was the day after Solomon and Isaac became Memory Masters again, we had made plans with other friends to have a play time at Commonground Park that morning. My mom decided to take the boys to the park so I could stay home with Casey.

At this point, I was thinking maybe Casey had the flu or food poisoning. Or maybe something like kidney stones. Certainly nothing life-threatening.

Casey's dad Gary came by around 10:00 a.m. to check on him. At that point, Casey had not gotten out of bed, but he had thrown up on his shirt and had wet the bed. In hindsight, I should have known that something was not right at that point, but I continued to think that Casey was just worn out from all the pressure he was under and maybe caught the flu in the process. Gary and I decided to continue to let him rest.

I cut the t-shirt off of him and he continued to sleep. Other than our initial discombobulated conversation at 4:30 that morning, Casey had not communicated since then, only slept.

It rained a little bit that morning, so the boys' playdate was cut short and not well attended. Grandma brought them back home, but before she left, she suggested I try to wake up Casey, in case she needed to take the boys home with her. I credit my mom with saving his life.

It was 11:30 a.m. now. I went into the bedroom and tried to wake Casey up. He was still breathing but, to my surprise, he was not responding to me at all.

I don't exactly remember the order of events, but I do remember going out to the kitchen to tell my mom Casey was not responding. I also told her I noticed his right hand in a fist and turned inward. At that point, she thought "stroke."

I must have called Gary next. His Allstate office was only a mile or so from our house, and he showed up very quickly.

He arrived while I was on the phone with the 9-1-1 operator who was telling me to get Casey off the bed and onto the floor. The operator told me not to worry about hurting Casey, just get him on the floor in case the paramedics needed to try to resuscitate him when they arrive.

Gary and I used the sheets of the bed to create a hammock that lifted Casey off the bed and onto the floor.

Of course, everything is a blur, but as I recall, within only a few minutes, our house was filled with firemen, paramedics, and policemen.

Solomon, who was eight at the time, recalls seeing the fire truck arrive first. That was a little confusing to him since he knew there wasn't a fire at the house. Solomon remembers that as Grandma gathered the boys and loaded them in her van, the last thing he saw was his dad being taken out of the house on a stretcher and placed in the ambulance.

I don't even remember what I communicated to the boys, but I think I told them that Daddy was obviously sick and needed to go to the hospital. I think I remember a policeman questioning me briefly on the occurrences of the morning—I suppose it was in order to be sure that no foul play occurred.

The ambulance left with Casey in the back. I packed some clothes for him with the hope that he would be returning home later that day. I gathered my belongings, and Gary drove me to the hospital.

I remember sending texts to Casey's closest friends, some of whom arrived at the hospital quickly.

Somehow I think Gary and I arrived at the hospital the same time the ambulance did. I wanted to go up to the ambulance as they took Casey out, but for some reason I didn't...maybe because I wasn't certain that was him and didn't want to be intrusive.

Gary, Casey's sister Rhea, and I waited somewhat patiently in the ER waiting room at Lakeland Regional Medical Center. Other close friends like our Pastor Mark Reynolds and his girlfriend Emma showed up, as well as Randy.

Gary had called his sister Scarlett, who was a nurse, and told her what was going on with Casey. She suggested he may have had a stress-related stroke. She herself had survived two such strokes, which gave me hope that Casey would be fine.

After about an hour, we were called back to a private waiting room. A physician spoke to us. I'm sure he spoke slowly and clearly, but the medical lingo was like a foreign language to me.

I'm really not sure what all I understood in those moments, but the doctor told us that Casey had suffered a major hemorrhagic stroke. Blood had leaked into his brain, and the CAT scan showed that the brainstem was pushed over due to the amount of blood that his brain was now holding.

The only option to extract the blood was brain surgery. It may have been that doctor or another one who mentioned that Casey may not be able to walk again or use any part of his right side, as a stroke can often affect the ability to move one side of the body. We were also told that Casey may not be able to speak or understand speech, since the area of his brain affected by the blood leakage controls his language. And of course, I'm sure I was told of the possibility of Casey not surviving this type of delicate brain surgery.

I have no idea how long the doctor talked with us. I don't ever remember seeing this doctor again. But after he left, those of us in the private waiting room gathered in a circle and prayed.

I suppose in many ways I was numb, I was processing, yet I remember strong moments of faith and strength that could only have been provided by the Spirit of God living in me.

After our prayer circle, we were able to go see Casey. He was obviously still unconscious, but now he was hooked up to IVs and monitors. His body was shaking and pulsating at times in an involuntary sort of way.

As we were there with him, other loved ones started showing up, including Pastor David McEntire, the pastor at First United Methodist Church, where Casey grew up and his parents still attended. David recalls hearing the prognosis from the neurosurgeon and recognizing the intensity and fragility of such a surgery.

Dr. Lau was Casey's neurosurgeon. He showed me the CAT scan and what he was intending to do. He informed me before signing the paperwork for surgery that if I chose no surgery, death was imminent. Of course, I signed the paperwork for permission for surgery.

My sister-in-law Laura works with a company that provides doctor's services. Although she and my brother Dave live in Ohio, she texted me information about various neurosurgeons in Lakeland, Florida. Her research recommended a different surgeon who apparently was not on call.

I asked Dr. Lau—who looked about eighteen—if he had ever performed surgeries like this. He assured me that he had, many more times than he would like to remember. That reassured me that he was the one to perform this surgery on my hubby. I know I prayed, and probably told Dr. Lau, that his hands would become the hands of Jesus performing this surgery on Casey.

I'm sure I kissed Casey goodbye, but honestly I don't remember specifics of that. I remember standing outside the area where he was, talking with Mark and Emma. A paramedic or firefighter who was in the ER was aware of Casey's diagnosis. I'm sure without realizing what he was doing, he spoke some very discouraging words about a friend of his that had suffered similarly to Casey and did not fare well. These words were not life to my spirit, but I remember keeping those words at a distance and not allowing them to corrupt my outlook on my current situation that I was still deeply processing.

At some point, we moved to the surgery waiting room where large monitors listed patients and their current status. Although it was around 4:30 p.m. by the time we left Casey for surgery, it seemed it took another hour or so before the screen indicated he was being prepped for surgery. Pastor David McEntire, who had sat with many family members during surgery days, explained his experience to be that the monitors don't always indicate the accurate time frame of what is actually happening. Nonetheless, we waited and prayed...waited and prayed.

I remember a simple, kind gesture from Mark and Emma that I just couldn't accept at the moment. They visited the hospital coffee shop and purchased a coffee or latte for me. It was immensely sweet of them! I felt bad about declining the cup, knowing I had absolutely no appetite for anything other than water. Emma was not at all offended by my refusal. In fact, she told me that in the days ahead, many people will offer things to me that may or may not be helpful...and that's okay.

As the afternoon progressed into evening, many family members and friends joined us in the waiting room to offer their support, love, and prayers for us. With the use of social media—particularly Facebook—

word of Casey's situation spread quickly among friends.

Many people started texting and messaging me regarding Casey. One text of a former pastor of ours arrived with a Scripture verse I clung to closely from Psalm 107:

> *Then they cried to the Lord in their trouble,*
> *and he saved them from their distress.*
> *He sent out his word and healed them;*
> *he rescued them from the grave (Psalm 107:19-20).*

I was definitely relying upon God and His Word to reach down and heal Casey from this devastating blow, just as we had done in the past as we encountered our plight regarding Selah and Cathy.

Waiting in the surgery waiting room, iPad in hand, I looked up Scriptures to pray and encourage my already weary soul. A friend saw me on my iPad and inquired about if I was researching about hemorrhagic strokes. Certainly, that would have been a reasonable thing to do at that moment, but my heart begged for peace and knew I could find that only in the words of my Savior.

We waited for at least a couple hours in the surgery waiting room. I'm not certain how long the actual surgery took, but it was near 7:00 p.m. when the neurosurgeon Dr. Lau came out to speak to the family.

A small circle joined around Dr. Lau, including me, Gary, Tee, and Rhea. Dr. Lau's disposition was pleasant and his body language was positive, which matched the report of Casey's surgery. Dr. Lau informed us that the surgery went very well, as he proceeded to hand me a small plastic bag that included Casey's wedding band. He was upbeat and positive about Casey up to this point, but he also pointed out that the next seventy-two hours were crucial in determining Casey's overall health and wholeness. In other words, we weren't out of the woods yet.

At this same time, dozens of people spontaneously gathered at Shepherd's Community Church to join in prayer for Casey. They shared their love and concern by making poster boards with prayers and get-well wishes on them. What a sweet group of people!

After our post-surgery meeting with Dr. Lau, we were allowed to go back and see Casey. He was placed in a medically-induced coma to allow his brain to rest. He was on a respirator, and the left side of his head was heavily bandaged. He had IVs and monitors on his arms and legs. Yet he rested very peacefully.

So very much had changed in the past twenty-four hours, yet I was so grateful that Casey had survived the first major step of this journey—brain surgery.

Mike Stasiak, our friend and head cook at First United Methodist Church in Lakeland, had been in the surgery waiting room with us. He left after a while to complete his duties for the Wednesday evening meal at FUMC, but he assured me he would be returning with food for us all.

Mike kept his word, bringing a meal and his famous bread pudding with him. The group that remained sat in the back area of the hospital cafeteria, enjoying the feast. As delicious as it was, I found it difficult to eat much of anything. My appetite had vanished. Mike informed me that I would often not want to eat in the days ahead, but I would have to eat to take care of myself. His wise words proved helpful in the coming days.

I don't remember specifics, but someone must have gone home to get me a change of clothes and toiletry items…or perhaps I went with someone to my house. At any rate, I spent the first night with Casey in the Trauma Intensive Care Unit. The hospital staff is not a big fan of family members spending the night in the ICU with their patients, and although they allowed me to stay, their sleeping arrangements communicated their lack of desire for me staying multiple nights. A sufficiently-cushioned reclining chair served as the "bed." The continuous involvement of the nurses in his care was superb, but the activity and the beeping monitors made for a restless night's sleep.

On my iPad, I had a playlist that included Scripture verses and teaching on healing. I asked the delightful nurse who was caring for him that night if it was okay for Casey to listen to these Scripture verses throughout the night. She agreed to my request and so I propped my iPad on his pillow and put the playlist on continuous repeat mode.

At the time, I had no idea how much trauma Casey's brain had been through that day. In hindsight, one might conclude that having someone talking in his ear all night long may have been detrimental to his brain healing. However, one might also suggest that all-night Scripture reading in his ear may have been the catalyst to Casey's progress.

In the whirlwind of activity, I honestly don't remember if I had any communication with our boys after Casey went to the hospital. I don't recall if they spent the night at Gary and Tee's house, or if Gerry stayed at our house with the boys. Either way, they were taken care of.

Despite the minimal sleep, I was grateful to be there in the room with Casey to ensure his safety and wellbeing. After that, I headed home for a shower and a much-needed nap.

In the days that followed, our amazing support system of family and friends rallied around me and took excellent care of me and our four young boys. This extraordinary community involved caretakers for our boys every day so I could spend the necessary time at the hospital with Casey. A sign-up sheet circulated around church members and homeschool families, and lo and behold, meals showed up at our home every other night!

Within a day or two, Pastor Mark contacted me because Gretchen Ceranic, Shepherd's children's director and our friend, wanted to set up a giving page for us to help with our expenses at this uncertain time. I had no idea how generous people would be to us, but let me just say that the giving community's generous gifts supported our family over the course of the next year!

One example of many occurred the Friday night following Casey's stroke. A fellow Classical Conversations family that lived not far from us had family in town and had extra food from their cookout. While their family was socializing, they discussed our family's situation. As a result of the conversation, they showed up at our door with delicious fresh grilled ribs—and a card from the sister-in-law of my friend. Inside this card, given from the generous heart and kindness of a person I still have never met, was a check for five hundred dollars!

As I opened the card, my eyes filled with tears and my heart filled with gratitude for God's amazing provision through the kindness of His people, many of whom I didn't even know.

At the root, I knew this to be a spiritual battle.

From the onset, I knew I had to fight for Casey in the spiritual realm—most specifically through prayer. In the days and weeks that followed, I circled our bed, praying Scripture and declaring my husband's healing. Through my prayers, I bound our enemy, the devil, from having any victory in Casey's life or body.

Even though I had the constant reminders of the fact that we prayed hard—and I mean hard—for Selah and Cathy, yet they both died, I knew I had to fight hard in prayer for Casey and his healing. So that's exactly what I did.

I fought hard for Casey through prayer, and let me tell you—prayer works!

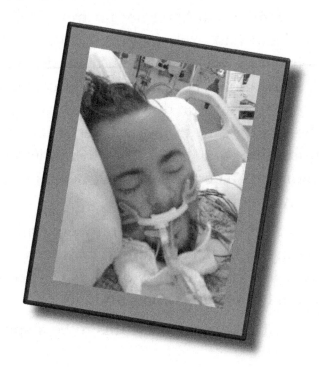

Quiet Strength of Healing

~ Our New Normal

At the consistent urging of Pastor David McEntire, Gary started a Caring Bridge page to document Casey's progress. Pastor David knew far too many families that wore themselves out trying to keep everyone informed on an individual basis regarding the progress—or lack thereof—of their loved one.

Casey's Caring Bridge website became the hub where posts were written by either Gary, Rhea, or me. Friends, family, and even acquaintances could sign up to receive an email each time a post was written. Since I was the primary writer and often times my updates were not posted until 11:00 p.m., friends and family would often stay up and wait for the report on Casey's day. Indeed, we had a great support system!

Four days after Casey's stroke, Gary wrote the first entry:

SATURDAY, APRIL 12, 2014

As many of you know, Casey experienced a large bleed on his brain causing a stroke on Wednesday, April 9. We have set up this account to help our family keep in contact with your family in regards to Casey's progress.

On Wednesday, we were shown the CT scan of Casey's brain and the large bleed on the left side. The Doctor was very clear about the potential of loss of use of arms and legs and the potential of loss of speech and the ability to understand speech.

After surgery to clear the blood, he was placed in what you could call a controlled coma to allow the brain to rest.

As I write, we have just returned home from the hospital now on Casey's fourth day in the Trauma ICU. He is still heavily sedated and on a ventilator to help him breathe. He is on all types of meds and on a feeding tube as of today. The doctors are continuing to monitor his blood pressure and the swelling in his brain. Casey also has some slight fluid in his lungs from where he aspirated some vomit during the onset of the stroke. He is receiving antibiotics and breathing treatments for this as well.

Casey has already amazed the doctors and his family. He is able to move his arms and legs and open his eyes. He is not currently following commands but hopefully that will come with time. He is frustrated at times with the ventilator and will try and reach to pull it out of his mouth, so his hands are restrained at all times. Today Casey opened his eyes wider than ever. His sister then started just talking to him and told him about his nice new haircut (looks like a Mohawk from where half was shaved during surgery) then Casey SMILED!!!!! It was amazing. Not a dry eye in the room. It was the sign we all needed. Casey is a fighter and is showing his strength every day.

The family asks for continued prayers. God is doing tremendous things and needs to be given the glory. Please continue to check back here for updates as well.

Today, as I read this entry, I am reminded of the dire and desperate situation we found ourselves in five years ago, and my heart is full of gratitude for how far Casey has progressed and what tremendous things God has done! He truly deserves all the glory!

Another memory of this Saturday was a much-needed outing with my boys. Up until this point and in the weeks that followed, our boys were being tossed around between grandparents, friends, homeschooling moms, babysitters, and just about anyone safe that I knew would take good care of them.

The Ice Cream Festival was happening that day at the Lakeland Linder Airport. Since we are avid fans of ice cream, it seemed like the perfectly fun outing we needed. I loaded up all four boys in the van and arranged to meet up with my friend Nicole Welch and her two kids.

As we pulled into the parking lot, I heard Isaac, age seven, say, "I wish Daddy were with us." I quickly added my agreement to his statement, wishing too that Daddy were with us to enjoy our time together as a family eating ice cream.

The festival included bounce houses, carnival-type games, a music stage, and a myriad of other activities and distractions. Of course, as we were there, I came across several friends who wanted to know the latest on Casey. I was already beginning to recognize the power of prayer in our situation, so I encouraged everyone who told me they were praying by saying that their prayers were working...so keep it up!

Our outing together as a family of five was indeed enjoyable. When we arrived home, the boys resumed their play activities, and Isaac brought his toys out to the couch.

His sweet, young processing mind was obviously working while he was playing because he randomly said out loud, "I hope Daddy doesn't die like Aunt Cathy, because then I would be without a daddy."

I walked over to him, hugged him and said, "Are you afraid of that?"

He said, "No, not really..."

I hugged him and reassured him that I too hoped his daddy would not die, realizing the reality of that particular moment that I could not assure him that his daddy would survive. I could only encourage him and love him, so that's what I did.

SUNDAY, APRIL 13, 2014

Pastor Mark Reynolds at Shepherd's Community UMC delivered a powerful message on the Sunday following Casey's stroke called "What Would Casey Say?" He spoke from the passage in Ephesians 6 that talks about the armor of God.

I watched the service online through livestream, as I wasn't quite ready to be bombarded by the love and the questions that would hit me on that morning by such a wonderful community. The simplicity of being home with my boys was very appealing.

The previous praise team from Shepherd's re-united for this particular Sunday. The church was packed, as people gathered in community at this time of uncertainty and extra reliance upon God. The team led the congregation in a powerful songs of declaration and faith.

Gary wrote this entry on Caring Bridge that evening:

Thank you. Those words are so inade-quate to express our gratitude to our commu-nity of "Casey's Army." Army may be the right word, for, as Pastor Mark Reynolds said this morning, we are standing side by side in this fight for Casey. By faith, I'm believing that the enemy has been defeated and victory is ours. I am humbled to feel your love and generosity of support for Casey, Cindy, and the boys. You guys are incredible.

Please continue your prayers. Specifi-cally for Casey's ability to swallow so the doc-tor can remove the ventilator and feeding tube. His blood pressure became too high to-day after the doctor's visit so prayers for a sta-ble and safe blood pressure are needed as well.

Here's the entry I posted on Caring Bridge:

We continue to give thanks and praise to Almighty God!

Today Casey was off sedation, so he was more awake and it was great to see his eyes! Some specific prayers would be for his blood pressure to be regulated so it doesn't go too high when he is stimulated.

Neurologist showed me all three CT scans. He said a couple times that the neurosurgeon did such a great job removing the blood clot from Casey's brain! And of course he did—those hands of the neurosurgeon were guided by the very hands of Jesus! :) That's another Praise the Lord! (PTL!) Another specific prayer concerning the CT scan would be that the Lord would heal any damage, especially in regards to vision/speech/comprehension.

Thanks so much for standing and believing with us! Keep the prayers, filled with faith, going up!

Cindy Cleveland, happily married to Casey

Fourteen years earlier, Casey and I spoke these words to each other as we committed our lives in marriage:

For better, for worse,
For richer, for poorer,
In sickness and in health,
To love and to cherish for as long as we both shall
live.

Before our wedding day, I remember contemplating the possibility of a "what if." What if something terrible happened to Casey, like a car accident? I remember wrestling with fear and wondering if I would remain committed to him, regardless of his physical situation or limitations. I asked myself, "Do I love Casey enough to stay by his side through sickness, disease, paralysis, and so forth?" Before saying the above vows, I decided I indeed loved him enough.

Now here we were, fourteen years later, living out our vows.

Although Casey was still on a ventilator, stuck in a hospital bed, unable to talk or even move much, I still decided to dress my best for him on our anniversary. I wore an adorable jeans outfit with my favorite red heels. They had been my sister Cathy's shoes, so they were extra special and extra cute! I'm sure I looked extra cute, too, that day, but since Casey's vision was so impaired—not realizing it at the time—I'm not certain he was aware of how cute I looked for him. Plus, those adorable red shoes that I wore around the hospital that day gave me a backache for two weeks! Yikes!

My parents and my sister Connie came to the hospital to visit Casey and to celebrate our anniversary with me.

I remember going to the hospital cafeteria for lunch. I sat by myself near a window, and even ate a dessert to celebrate our anniversary...by myself.

Upon returning to his room, I played some love songs from my iPad for Casey, one of which was a song that we danced to at our wedding reception before leaving for our honeymoon. The song is titled "Spinning Like a Wheel" sung by Susan Ashton.

Although not a very popular song, it was a special one for Casey and me. I loved on him as best I could while the song played, which meant putting my face up by his face and stroking his hair. At some point he opened his eyes and gave me the best anniversary gift he could have given me on that day, as described here in my evening post:

> Casey gave me the most amazing anniversary gift ever!!! Today we celebrated our

fourteenth wedding anniversary, and he was lying still in a hospital bed most of the day. The doctor informed us that in order for the ventilator to be removed, Casey needed to be more alert. They stopped all sedation and drip meds yesterday, and inserted a pic line today. This afternoon, it became obvious that the sedation was flowing out of his system and he started to be more alert! Now, remember in yesterday's post, I mentioned the neurologist told me of the damage done on his brain in regards to comprehension and understanding. Well, we started asking him questions, and he was making effort to communicate his answers. The moment that made our anniversary complete was when I said, "Babe, do you know I love you?" and he nodded his head "Yes." Of course, I started to weep, and he looked at me! I assured him these were tears of joy!

Sooooo many people have mentioned they are praying for Casey, and I tell them to keep it up. The prayers are working!

Specific prayers:
• continue to be for his blood pressure to stay at good levels,
• for wisdom for the doctors to know when to remove the ventilator,

• for safety over his vocal cords in regards to the ventilator, as well as no infections,
• for his ability to swallow once the ventilator is removed,
• for continued progress and complete healing for Casey's brain, body, and soul.

Thank you for fighting this battle with us!

Cindy, happily married to Casey

And if the Spirit of him who raised Jesus from the dead is living in you, he who raised Christ from the dead will also give life to your mortal bodies because of his Spirit who lives in you (Romans 8:11 NIV).

Rhea came for a visit in the afternoon, so she had more to add about the details of the day:

So I am going to add to Cindy's post from yesterday. These are the non-sappy details, Lol.

Casey was amazing today. He was more awake as the sedation slowly continues to work itself out of his body. Around 3:00 the staff came in and added a pic line into his arm and were able to take out all of his other IV lines. This is a good thing because as he moves more the lines were getting pulled and becoming tangled and now we don't have to worry about that at all.

Then around 6:00, Casey opened his eyes again. This time we started talking to him and he actually interacted with us. It was so uplifting. We asked him if he knew what had happened to him and he shrugged his shoulder. We again explained where he was and what had happened. Cindy then explained to him that he will be healed in the name of Jesus and that so many people are praying for him. She reminded him what a man of God he was. She asked him if he knew that. He nodded YES.

The nurse (Jessie, who was fantastic today) was in there for all of this, then asked Casey if she could please suction out his mouth. He nodded yes to her. He absolutely hates the suction but was unusually calm while she did it. It was almost as if since he said it was okay then he was more relaxed. However, he started coughing and since the fluid in his lungs is slowly working itself up she had to clean the ventilator tube itself. This is a more invasive procedure and makes Casey gag. The nurse told Casey what had to be done and he started shaking his head back and forth NO. He also reached up his right arm to grab her hand to stop her. This was huge. This was the first time he actually moved his right arm with purpose on his own instead of just in response to the doctor pinching him. It also means that he does understand what we are saying to him and what is going on around him. The doctor had told us that he thought Casey would have a very hard time with comprehension, but that was proven wrong today.

Casey was also using his left arm a lot today. He scratched his own goatee and pulled his left knee all the way up and scratched his leg too. He held his arm in the air for a while and just looked at it. We also put the capo that Emily, one of the praise band members, dropped off for him in his hand and he played with that for a bit and was even able to squeeze it.

The nurses and doctors are continuing to monitor his blood pressure. They are also trying to wean him off the ventilator. The bandage has been taken off his head and his surgery site is healing nicely. Our goal is to get the tubes out of his mouth. That will relieve a lot of his discomfort and agitation. The occupational and physical therapists are continuing to work with him as well.

Casey is making great gains. Please continue to pray.

I finished the day with a simple post on Facebook:

I'm a different woman than I was last Tuesday night....

After all, last Tuesday, life was full but for the most part "normal." I went to bed last week with four boys sleeping soundly and a husband who lay in the bed beside me.

This week, my husband slept in a hospital bed and our boys were being juggled around from one kindhearted person to another.

This week, I was astounded by the generous grace of God and His infinite care for me and my family.

Out of the thirty people that commented on my post, I think my favorite comment came from my brother-in-law Charles Asbridge:

Praise God! Most Christians live their lives and never know the true feeling of being held by Jesus! And here's the good news...even after Casey is completely restored you'll never be the same again!

How true his words are! There's nothing like being held by the strong arms of Jesus! Although I have not chosen this challenging road to walk down, I have seen God's goodness and felt His love in a way that makes the journey worth traveling.

Charles is right: I have never been the same, and that's a good thing!

WEDNESDAY, APRIL 16, 2014

We met many precious people through our experience in the TICU.

As demonstrated in Wednesday's post, it was a very exciting day:

> Today started out with the exciting news that Casey had pulled the ventilator out of his mouth! That's right—he was done with it, and in a brief moment when the nurse was out of the room, he pulled it out and was holding it when she walked back in! (A nurse-friend on the same unit said, "We nurses don't like to admit it, but that really is a good thing. The fact he had the strength, ability, and determination to pull it out is really good.") His breathing continued to be strong, so the vent has stayed out today. PTL! He was also very awake for nearly two hours! We would ask him questions like, "Can you see me?" He nodded yes. "Am I blurry?" He nodded yes. He answered, "Yeh" to the nurse, and was trying to speak, but it usually takes a little while to be able to speak

once the ventilator comes out. But I think he said, "Drink of water," so I asked him, "Do you want a drink of water?" and he nodded yes!

By the time the doctors came to assess him, he was worn out, so they didn't get to see his progress like we did. He also had an MRI done today.

Specific prayers would include:
- be more alert,
- pass his swallow test,
- cough the secretions out,
- KEEP the ventilator out,
- blood pressure regulated,
- MRI = good report,
- COMPLETE healing of his brain, body, and soul
- COMPLETE healing for others we've met in TICU, young and old.

Thanks so much for fighting this battle with us, Army of God!

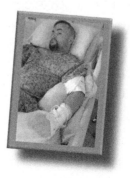

THURSDAY, APRIL 17, 2014

The best way to talk about this day is to read it from my Caring Bridge entry:

> Today brought more surprises and more progress. Remember yesterday, Casey pulled out—on his own—the ventilator and feeding tube. He stayed strong enough to keep the ventilator out (PTL!), and they placed a feeding tube down his nose. I believe the nurse was nice enough to allow his left arm (the one he favors right now) to be unrestrained, so she put a padded-type mitten on his left hand so he wouldn't scratch at the large wound on his head that is healing so nicely. Well, apparently Casey had had enough of the mitten, so by placing the mitten between the backside of his knee and thigh of his left leg, he was able to pull the mitten off, and then proceeded to pull the feeding tube out of his nose!!! That's our determined Casey! He has not passed the swallow test yet, but the speech therapist will come in the morning to assess him again. If he passes the swallow test, he will start eating liquid foods. If not, they'll have to put a feeding tube down his nose again (which he obviously doesn't like), or directly into his stomach (which he

probably won't like either).

Casey started talking quite a bit today! Some things made sense, some things didn't. But from what I understand, the nurse noticed improvement with his speech, even from this morning! Rhea, his sister, was able to talk to him about our boys, and she said he started crying, tears running down his face. She hugged him, and he lifted his RIGHT ARM up and squeezed her arm!

Here's another cool thing…Casey started SINGING today! Rhea played the song "My Savior Lives" by Aaron Shust, and he started singing along. Some of the words were jumbled up, but he's still got pitch and beat!!!

Folks, do you see what's happening here?!?! The best word I can use to describe this is—Miracle!!! Let's think about this: eight days ago, we were told Casey may be paralyzed from the neck down; four days ago, I was told, according to the CT scan, he would not understand us, and I'm fairly certain the doctor was not very optimistic about his ability to speak. Well, so far, in these few, yet very loooonnng days, we're witnessing something very different! Something very miraculous! And to God be the glory! Does Casey have a long road of recovery ahead? Yes he does. But the same God who has helped us through these past eight days will help us through the months ahead. If you don't know this powerful God who dwells within Casey and is giving life to his flesh (according to Romans 8:11), you need to know Him! His God is so worth knowing!!!

Specific prayer points:
• Casey be alert and pass his swallow test tomorrow,
• continue to keep his blood pressure at a healthy level,
• COMPLETE healing for his brain, body, and soul,
• divine wisdom for doctors, nurses, therapists, and all caring for Casey,
• his brain would be able to "connect the dots" when speaking and when moving his right side,
• vision be perfect,
• for our four boys as Rhea and I talk to them tomorrow about Daddy's healing process. (All they basically know is Daddy is sick and at the hospital getting better.) Pray that they won't be fearful, and that they will embrace Daddy's condition until he's 100%!

We can't possibly thank you enough for standing with us, praying, and believing for Casey's TOTAL recovery! The prayers of faith are working, so keep it up, Casey's "Army of God"!

YOU WILL KEEP IN PERFECT PEACE THOSE WHOSE MINDS ARE STEADFAST, BECAUSE THEY TRUST IN YOU. TRUST IN THE LORD FOREVER, FOR THE LORD, THE LORD HIMSELF, IS THE ROCK ETERNAL (ISAIAH 26:3, 4 NIV).

FRIDAY, APRIL 18, 2014 (GOOD FRIDAY)

Scripture is such a powerful tool. That's why I had Casey listen to it all night long after his brain surgery the night of his stroke. I liked closing each of my Caring Bridge journal entries with a Scripture that Casey's Army of God could pray in agreement with me. Romans 8:11 was my go-to Scripture on any given day, but the Bible has plenty of other verses that encouraged me in one way or another at this time. So as you'll see, I start including other verses to close out my journal entries.

<u>Miracle Man: Day 9</u>

I promise not to make this entry as long as last night's. :) I could just say Casey had another great day of progress, but you probably want more details than that. Casey was much more alert today, and he was talking A LOT! It seemed to me that he would say something that didn't make sense, and then pause or laugh because he knew what he was trying to say wasn't coming out right. I'm sure he was getting a bit frustrated, but he handled it all very well. We kept reassuring him that he's doing such a great job, certainly much more than the doctors expected at this time.

Speaking of doctors, Rhea sat down with the neurologist and saw Casey's MRI. All the doctor could say was, and I quote, "remarkable improvement." Shall we say "Miracle"?!?! I told that same doctor on Monday that God was going to heal Casey completely, and that he is a Miracle Man! Go God!!!

Casey had physical therapy again today, and he got to sit in a chair for the first time. The PT was very pleased with his progress even from two days ago.

To add to the activities of the week, as I was leaving the hospital this afternoon, a kind gentleman got out of his car at a red light to inform me that I was driving on a flat tire. I pulled over, and two very kind gentlemen changed the tire for me. And then for more kindness…Gary took the vehicle to B and L Tires in Lakeland, and they had heard about Casey's stroke, so they didn't charge us anything for fixing the tire! So, if you're in the Lakeland area, be sure to support B and L Tires. They're good people! :)

Specific prayer points:
• COMPLETE healing for Casey's brain, body, and soul,
• that his brain would make the proper connections when trying to speak and sing,
• vision be perfect,
• pass swallow test,
• divine wisdom for all caring for him,
• that our boys would have a positive experience when we go to visit Daddy this weekend.

Thanks for your prayers for Rhea and me as we talked to the boys today. They received the news about Daddy very well, and we plan to visit him tomorrow and/or Sunday.

Good night, Casey's Army of God!

But he was pierced for our transgressions, he was crushed for our iniquities; the punishment that brought us peace was on him, and by his wounds we are healed (Isaiah 53:5 NIV).

SATURDAY, APRIL 19, 2014

At LRMC, the nurses' shifts spanned twelve hours: from 7:00 a.m. to 7:00 pm and from 7:00 p.m. to 7:00 a.m. This meant that if I wanted to know how Casey did through the night, I would need to call by 6:30 a.m. to speak with the night nurse. On this particular Saturday morning, I was able to call and talk to his nurse, and she gave me a good report, so I wrote this bonus journal entry right away.

<u>Miracle Man: Night 9</u>

I just talked to Casey's night nurse, Stephanie, and couldn't help but write about her report. She said he had a good night. One of the nurses played Christian worship music on her phone, and he was in there singing and worshiping his Great God! Stephanie said he did not get all the words, but he was definitely singing and humming on pitch. She said, "We had our own Good Friday service in here; we were all so blessed by him!" He kept saying, "This is good! This is good!"

I hope this blesses your day like it does mine!

Keep the prayers going....they're work-ing!

I will extol the Lord at all times; his praise will al-ways be on my lips. I will glory in the Lord; let the afflicted hear and rejoice. Glorify the Lord with me; let us exalt his name together. Taste and see that the Lord is good; blessed is the one who takes refuge in him (Psalm 34:1-3, 8 NIV).

Since this was the day before Easter, Shepherd's Community had an egg hunt and fun activities for the kids. It was so good to be with these friends and believ-ers in Christ who were standing in faith for Casey's complete healing.

The boys enjoyed the Easter egg hunt and bounce house. From there we loaded them up to go see Daddy in the hospital for the first time. Gerry Hubbs followed us there so she could help out. She also took some videos of Casey and his reunion with his boys.

He must have started to piece his life back to-gether because apparently he did not remember that he had a family, but as soon as he saw these four bois-terous blessings, he declared, "There's my boys!"

Hugs and kisses were exchanged and even a few silly moments. Casey attempted to say their names, but that would come in time...not this day. And the boys seemed okay with that. They were just glad to see their daddy again, and that's really all that mattered.

In preparation for Easter Sunday, Casey and his awesome team had been working extra hard to finish the new stage, sound, and lighting systems at Shepherd's Community Church. The project was almost complete when Casey had his stroke.

If I remember correctly, the night after Casey's stroke, I received a late night text which was a picture of the new stage. To honor Casey, his awesome team, which included Randy (sound), Kyle (video), and even Gary, along with a few other wonderful volunteers, came together to complete the project, and it looked amazing!

The boys and I awoke early to get ready on this celebratory day. The generous ladies at Shepherd's had created an Easter basket for each of our boys, so that added to the excitement of the morning. (This was after already receiving huge Easter baskets the night before from Gary and Tee's friends, the Feddelers.) Our neighbor at the time, Alicia Bryant Baker, came over early to help get the boys dressed and ready.

The Praise Team at Shepherd's did a great job stepping up and taking over the musical responsibilities for Easter Sunday. I was scheduled to sing the special, which was Darlene Zschech's song "Victor's Crown." As I sang, I remember feeling such power and conviction for the victory we have as believers in Jesus

Christ. Because Jesus conquered death, hell, and the grave, He wears the Victor's Crown. And because we believe in Him, we too are "more than conquerors" (Romans 8:37).

Yes, my husband lay in a hospital bed.

Yes, an amazing amount of uncertainty lay before us.

Yes, my life had been forever changed as a result of Casey's stroke.

And yes, my Savior and Lover of my Soul wears the Victor's Crown and I have much to celebrate!

And celebrate we did! After the church service, we enjoyed lunch at Gary and Tee's house before taking the boys back to the hospital to visit Casey.

This journal entry was written by Gary and shares a little bit about our time with Casey.

Miracle Man Day 11
Journal entry by Gary Cleveland

So Casey had another good day. The nurses are regularly moving him into a reclining chair so he can get out of the bed and sit up more. He is continuing to talk a lot. Some of his thoughts are jumbled but some are crystal clear. He seems to know what he wants to say and if he can't get the right word out he will start making random noises and laughing. He definitely has his same sense of humor. Cindy has brought his boys up to see him twice now. He can't remember names very well but he said, "There's my boys." He gave them hugs and kisses and was making faces at Josiah just like before.

He is starting to use his right hand more and even move his right leg some. He says how weird it all is because he can't really feel his right side very well but he sees it moving. Every day Casey is getting stronger and gaining more confidence and is expressing how he feels and what he wants.

The doctor will hopefully put in a peg tube tomorrow (feeding tube that goes directly into his stomach). He hasn't had any real nutrition since early Friday morning when he pulled out the last attempt at a feeding tube. The peg tube will be put directly into the stomach and then covered with a band almost like a back brace so he won't stand a chance of pulling it out. [Note: the peg tube never needed to be inserted; praise the Lord!]

Please continue to pray as God continues to work his miracle. Casey is a fighter as well and every day we see improvement. He has a long way to go but think of how far he has already come. It's amazing!

The pages ahead hold a summary of our journey from April 2014 until the present. If you wish to read more day-to-day details, they are listed in the Caring Bridge Journal Entries Appendix at the back of this book.

On Day 15 of this journey, Casey was released from TICU to a regular hospital room. Although we were delighted with his progress, we were also nervous about his new-found "freedom." Casey was not yet able to get up and use the bathroom by himself, nor was he completely able to understand how to use the nurses' call button when he needed someone. The nurses in the TICU were absolutely amazing: monitoring him, watching his every move (except when he pulled out his breathing tube and feeding tube!), and taking such good care of him. Yet the nurses in the regular hospital room, although very wonderful, did not watch his every move, which made us family members a bit nervous.

By Day 19, Casey transferred from the hospital to an inpatient rehab center in Winter Haven. Once again, although we were elated at his continued progress, a time of adjustment for us all ensued as he transitioned to this new place. Once he got settled, multiple therapies started every day: physical, occupational, and speech.

The day we saw Casey walking on his own for the first time was more than exciting! Casey's parents and I attended that physical therapy session, and tears rolled down our faces! Casey had come so far, and we were so grateful!

Occupational therapy worked on his right hand so it could strengthen and function normally, even though he couldn't feel it normally. The day I received the okay to bring in his guitar was a bittersweet experience. He was thrilled to be holding his guitar again after several weeks, but because he couldn't feel his right hand, he couldn't feel the guitar pick used to strum his guitar and make the beautiful music he was so used to hearing from his instrument. The first few sessions with his guitar were not very long to keep him from getting too frustrated with his limitations.

Speech therapy was the most demanding and involved. I recall sitting in his sessions. Pam, the therapist, had picture cards sitting on the table. Each one contained a picture of simple words we say every day: cat, dog, table, chair, shoe, shirt. Casey attempted to say each picture's word. This was no easy task for a person suffering from aphasia.

Here's a little exercise for us: Consider any simple word that you use on a regular basis, and imagine not being able to say that word. What would you do? You would probably do what Casey did regularly—he figured out another way to communicate what he was trying to say by the use of hand motions (or eventually trying to spell the word), or he just gave up until another time.

Casey recalls learning to say the word "tea." He enjoys a glass of tea with his lunch or dinner, yet he was unable to ask for tea because he could not say the word. He remembers the delight of finally being able to enjoy a glass of tea because now he could actually ask for one.

After three and a half weeks at the inpatient rehab center, and exactly six weeks after his stroke (Day 42), Casey was finally able to come home! What a day of rejoicing that was!

Once again, we had a major adjustment period, working together with Casey, his parents, and the boys, to figure out what worked and what didn't work well in our "new normal." Nonetheless, we were thrilled to finally have Daddy back home with us as he continued to work hard and experience the miraculous touch of our great God!

Casey was not able to be home alone for quite some time. He came home on May 21, so we had the summer months to adjust to our new normal.

In June, I met with a couple who has loved on us in various ways over the years. This time, as I sought their advice on some financial issues, a conversation regarding schooling for the boys came up. I told them I was planning to continue homeschooling...after all, that's what I do: I teach. In this meeting, I was encouraged to consider putting the boys into school, in order to give Casey time for rest and quiet, so his brain could continue to heal.

Over the next week, whenever I thought about school for the boys, I cried. Through my tears, I would talk to God and say, "Lord, I don't know where You want them to go to school, so please show me what we are to do."

Keep in mind that conversations with Casey were very limited. The aphasia kept him from understanding or following any conversation well. To consult with Casey about a school decision was not something I could do. I could tell him I was considering different options for school, but to have him help me brainstorm or discuss our options was impossible at this point.

Three weeks after the school conversation began, I was contacted by Andrea Payne. Andrea worked as a teacher at First Methodist School in Bartow, and she was a dear friend of Rhea, so Andrea had been a good encouragement to Rhea during Casey's stroke and recovery. Additionally, I had taught music to Andrea's kids when they were young.

Andrea had called to see if I would be willing to teach music two days a week at First Methodist School. This position would also allow our four boys to attend the school, which provided education for two-year-olds through eighth graders.

Working two days a week would allow me to have three days to take Casey to therapies and doctor's appointments. Since the boys would be at school every day, this arrangement would give Casey some quiet time during the day for rest and continued healing.

A couple little hiccups along the way kept us uncertain as to whether this arrangement was going to actually work out or not, but in typical God-style, He came through in amazing ways and we were off to school!

Since Casey couldn't be home alone yet, his mom, dad, or a friend would hang with him or take him to lunch on the days I was teaching.

He continued outpatient therapies for several weeks—first graduating from physical therapy, then occupational therapy. I don't recall the specifics, but Casey's speech therapy was covered under a charity grant, so after a year of outpatient speech therapy, he was asked to conclude his sessions. Although he had come so far in his communication over that year, he still had a long way to go.

One specific memory I have of a speech therapy session occurred in the beginning of November. For as long as I had known Casey, he sang a beautiful version of "O Holy Night" every Christmas Eve. At first it was at Manatee United Methodist Church in Bradenton, where his parents had grown up and his extended family continued to attend. In more recent years, he would sing it at whatever congregation we were participating in or leading worship for. Of course, people heard of his beautiful singing, so he was asked to sing "O Holy Night" at Christmas parties and family gatherings. We just couldn't get enough of it!

Just days after his stroke, when Casey lay in the hospital bed on life support, his parents, Pastor Mark, and I made a faith statement: "Casey will sing 'O Holy Night' again this Christmas!"

So here he is in speech therapy, desiring to work on the song in preparation for Christmas coming. It's early November, nearly six weeks before his first scheduled performance. Through his aphasia, he struggled with every word, taking nearly the whole forty-five-minute therapy session to read through the two verses and two choruses of this most beloved Christmas song.

Through his own sweat and tears—and God's grace—Casey performed "O Holy Night" at the Christmas Eve service at Shepherd's Community United Methodist Church, only eight months post-stroke. Although not a flawless performance, it was absolutely beautiful—and a testament to the God who still today causes the weary world to rejoice with a thrill of hope.

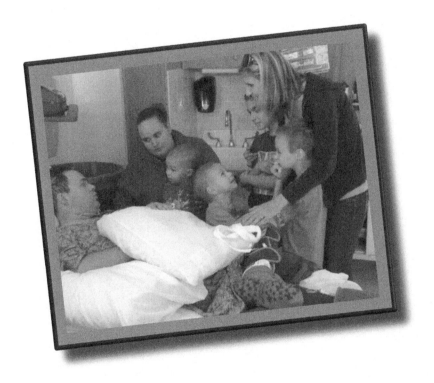

159

Quiet Strength Through Perseverance

~ Whatever It Takes

It did not take us long to figure out that Casey was going to be out of commission for a while, especially in regards to providing financially for our family. Yet, even through this unexpected, uncertain journey I found myself on, I also saw God's faithful provision and prevenient grace.

Within the first couple weeks after Casey's stroke, Pastor Mark asked if I wanted to take over as Worship Leader at Shepherd's until Casey was able again. I was certainly grateful for this opportunity to lead the praise team and I graciously accepted.

As God has faithfully done—over and over and over again—He provided the time, energy, and strength to take on this responsibility. Although it was only ten hours a week, I needed all the strength I could get to juggle all the other responsibilities that I was now faced with.

Thursday evening rehearsals proved a sweet time for me. We gathered as a band, worked on songs for the upcoming Sundays, and worshiped our great God together...yes, even at rehearsals! This fabulous team of supporters loved Casey so much and were excited each week to hear what God was doing in Casey's healing process.

Sunday mornings were full—getting the boys up and ready all by myself—but we all survived. Shepherd's agreed to pay a childcare worker to watch the boys during our Sunday morning rehearsal time. That was huge! I could run rehearsal without fear of what my little ones were doing because they were being well taken care of.

On Mother's Day, Casey and his dad were able to watch the service via livestream, as he was still at the rehab center. If I remember correctly, that was the Sunday we introduced Bethel Church's version of "It Is Well," one that we still love to lead today. I was introduced to this song after Casey's stroke and was immediately drawn to the beauty of the music and the lyrics. And like the hymn, the song concludes by declaring, "It is well, it is well with my soul."

I remember the Thursday night Casey was able to join us at rehearsal for the first time. Rhea brought him, knowing he probably would not be able to last through the whole rehearsal. Not only was it late for him, but also the loud music could easily overstimulate him. Of course, he was delighted to be there, and everyone was thrilled to see him.

Eventually, Casey was able to attend his first worship service on a Sunday morning. He sat on the front row through the whole service, taking in all the sights and sounds. I recall the conversation I had with him on the ride home. He was discouraged because, due to the aphasia, he was unable to understand Pastor Mark's words as he taught. I attempted to encourage him by saying that although he could not understand Mark today, one day, when he's healed and can understand, we will look back and celebrate how far Casey has come.

And that's exactly what we have done!

Not too many weeks later, Casey reached a major milestone by playing his guitar as part of the praise team at Shepherd's. This was his first time being on stage with the team since his stroke. Of course, before his stroke, he was the worship leader, so we were all overjoyed to have him part of the team again! Although the words of the songs didn't come quickly enough for him yet, he was able to beautifully worship the Lord with his guitar as we all rejoiced at his miracle unfolding before us! To God be the glory.

Dr. Todd Robinson strongly recommended hyperbaric oxygen therapy to help aid Casey's brain in the healing process. The best option at that time was to travel to Winter Park every day for four weeks. To make the most of this experience, each week one of the boys would travel with us and have a special outing with Daddy and Mommy. After the therapy session, we would go for lunch or ice cream together. We have sweet memories and pictures of those outings.

During those hour-and-a-half trips on I-4, I recall driving by Gaylord Palms and praying God would provide a way for our family to enjoy some time there. As the summer of 2014 came to a close, our family was blessed with a mini-vacation at the beautiful and prestigious Gaylord Palms in Orlando. (See the details of our trip in Appendix I ~ Caring Bridge Journal Entries on Casey's Journey.)

Then the three older boys were off to school at First Methodist School in Bartow. Solomon started third grade with the beloved and beautiful Mrs. Elsa. Isaac began in second grade with sweet Mrs. Wolfe. Daniel was in the three-year-old class with endearing and lovable Mrs. Janie. Josiah joined the school once he turned two years old in October, and his excellent teacher was Mrs. Serena.

Two days a week, I taught music classes at FMS to all the students in the school, two-year-olds through eighth grade. I enjoyed being in the classroom again, developing my own music curriculum and preparing students for performances throughout the year.

By the time our wonderful first year at FMS was coming to a close, my conversations with the Lord about our financial situation began to express some concern. I knew He had been so faithful to provide through this first year of transition following Casey's stroke. His provision came through my two part-time jobs (worship leading and teaching), as well as through the kindness and generosity of people who gave to us following Casey's stroke. As our financial cushion depleted, we needed another source of income. And that's exactly what God provided!

A position to teach private piano lessons at Geneva Classical Academy came to my attention. This was an excellent opportunity because I could teach during the school day, choosing my own hours and price. The school would take care of the marketing and scheduling. And to this day, Geneva's staff, students, and parents have been a delight to work with. Obviously, Geneva was part of God's faithful provision for us.

At the same time, I accepted another part-time music teaching position, which was only one afternoon a week at Magnolia Montessori Academy, teaching general music classes to all their students in kindergarten through sixth grade. I was able to teach much of the same material I was using at FMS, so once again, we saw God's provision and strength.

Yet this meant I was juggling all the family responsibilities and four part-time jobs!

By this time, Casey was able to stay at the house by himself on the days I was working. The other days were spent grocery shopping, going to the doctor's office, and occasionally enjoying a lunch date together.

At the writing of this book, we are five years post-stroke. Our boys recently started their third year at Lakeland Christian School. Each school year, we seek the Lord for His guidance concerning where He would like our boys to attend. Each year, He has made beautifully clear where they should go, even if it is last-minute.

On this journey of trust, each year my job responsibilities look slightly different than the year before. In fact, I recently took on another part-time job as Assistant Worship Leader at First United Methodist Church in Lakeland. In addition to worship leading and teaching, I enjoy each opportunity I am given to share our story of God's faithfulness to us.

Multiple jobs. School changes. Family responsibilities. Speaking opportunities. Writing a book. Through it all, God has been incredibly faithful to provide the strength and perseverance needed for this journey. And for this, I give Him great thanks!

QUIET STRENGTH OF PURPOSE

~ DISCOVERING PURPOSE FOR THE PAIN

Part of my healing process after Selah was born was recognizing the good that has come from her death. I began to realize that any good that comes from her passing was giving purpose to our pain. It made me feel like her death was not in vain but had a purpose, although at times very difficult to recognize.

I have chosen—and it's a choice—not to become bitter and angry at God for my pain. Rather, with each loss, I have chosen to cling to my God who has supported me, strengthened me, and given me grace to take the next step along this uncertain journey. I have chosen to become better, not bitter.

Certain songs and lyrics mean more to me now as a worship leader because of what we have experienced.

I remember hearing the worship song "Oceans" by Hillsong on the radio while Casey was still in the hospital. We had led that song many times prior to Casey's stroke, but now, upon hearing those lyrics, I sat in my vehicle in the hospital parking garage and cried like a baby. The lyrics ask the Holy Spirit to take us deeper in our faith—deeper than we would ever go on our own—knowing that depth makes our faith stronger.

I believe our pain and loss have taken our praise to the next level. As Casey and I worship our great God, the words are not empty, but deep and meaningful. Such a gift gives purpose to our pain.

Since our boys have walked the journey of pain and transition with us, they too have seen the faithfulness of God in their own lives. Following Selah's entrance into heaven, I had a sense that our boys would have a greater understanding of and anticipation for heaven.

As our boys' musical talents and love for the Lord have grown, we have enjoyed opportunities to lead worship together as a family, which is such a blessing and a joy! To date, our boys have led worship with us at women's retreats, women's events, church services, and various mini-concerts. There's something incredibly beautiful and powerful about worshiping our great God and looking across the stage to see our children using their talents to worship the God they know to be faithful and true to them, even in their young lives.

I'm not certain our boys would be as mature in their faith had we not experienced what we have and responded to it as we have. I'm grateful for the Lord's purposes being fulfilled in all of our lives.

I am encouraged by the truth found in the first chapter of Philippians in the Amplified Bible:

I am convinced and confident of this very thing, that He who has begun a good work in you will [continue to] perfect and complete it until the day of Christ Jesus [the time of His return] (Philippians 1:6 AMP).

That verse tells me that even though my sister Cathy has passed from this earth, the good work God started in her continues through her children, continues through her family, continues through those she touched, and all of that good work will continue until the day Jesus returns! That promise gives me great hope and encouragement, and it helps me to find purpose in our pain and loss.

Consider this promise from Romans 8 in the Amplified Bible:

And we know [with great confidence] that God [who is deeply concerned about us] causes all things to work together [as a plan] for good for those who love God, to those who are called according to His plan and purpose (Romans 8:28 AMP).

God has a plan and purpose for my life and yours. We may not fully understand it. We may not even have the slightest conception of what it is. But this I know…His plan and purpose for my life and your life are for good. Jeremiah 29:11 tells us:

"For I know the plans I have for you," declares the Lord, "plans to prosper you and not to harm you, plans to give you hope and a future" (Jeremiah 29:11).

Believing God has a good plan for my life, understanding that He is able to work out good in all circumstances, and trusting that He will carry out this good plan even after I am off this earth gives me hope. Such truth gives me purpose for my pain.

How about you?

QUIET STRENGTH OF PEACE
~ HEAVEN EXPERIENCE

At some point during Casey's hemorrhagic stroke or brain surgery, when life was spinning out of control for me, he was having a quite different experience. I call it an "experience" because he was moving somewhere, yet he never saw anyone. I'm going to let Casey explain his experience in his own words.

I remember feeling sick while I was sleeping. That's when I felt a lot of heat; I was really hot. I felt like I was going to throw up and needed to get to the bathroom, but I couldn't.

I opened my eyes just slightly, but that's when I saw darkness everywhere. Full darkness, yet all of a sudden there was a light that appeared on my right side. Then I realized that there was something over there, kind of far away, so I thought, "I'll go and check this out."

So I went over and that's when this light was a big round area, a big light that was a veil of light. Very soft looking, all white, but very strong and bright. I was able to see it, and I knew I was moving toward it. I don't know if I was walking, but I knew I was moving toward it.

I thought I was moving into the light, but that's when I realized there were two hands that came through the light and touched me on my chest. Very soft. Instantly, I felt, "Just hang out, everything's cool."

Then all of a sudden, it poured all over me. It was growing in my body, inside of me, outside of me, it was all over me...peace.

YOU DON'T KNOW WHAT FEAR IS BECAUSE YOU LIVE IN IT EVERY DAY.

Instantly, I could feel the fear being ripped off of me. Quick. It was gone. Anything I ever experienced. In that moment, I was free.

So I was right in this peace. This peace was all over me. I remember the feeling of it was like I had been with a great friend. A lot of peace. I was safe. I knew Jesus was right in front of me. I didn't see Him, but I knew Jesus was with me.

I was there for quite a while. I didn't say a word. I'm sure I was smiling a lot. I was just waiting there, not sure what I was waiting for, but it didn't much matter at all. I didn't care who I was or what I had to do, or feel like I had lost anything, or like I was busy. All of that was gone. I was in the completeness of peace but it was so strong!

I could feel the strength of the peace. It's like I could be there a thousand years, no big deal.

At some point, I knew I was leaving. It was like I was stepping backward almost. I could feel my body coming back. And I was jumping back into this darkness, and I could feel the fear coming back. Eventually, I knew I was back, and that's when I realized I was in the hospital. And instantly, I could feel all the weight and the pain, and the stepping back of all the issues of my body.

Every day that my body gets better, I feel farther and farther away from Jesus. It makes me very sad. I have to remind myself how close I was with Him.

Here's the irony: when we're here on this earth, we say we are "alive." And when someone passes on from this earth, we say they are "dead." Yet, those that "die" and know Jesus as their Savior are more "alive" than we are here on this earth.

WHEN YOU'RE "DEAD," YOU'RE LITERALLY MORE "ALIVE."

That's why death has no sting.
1 Corinthians 15:55 says:

"Where, O death, is your victory?
Where, O death, is your sting?"

Death has no sting. It is true.

Being in the presence of Jesus equals complete peace—no fear. Now I call that "real life"!

I want people to know that being busy with their jobs—what I like to call Professional Busyness—does not really matter. How important you are doesn't matter. Busyness…it does not matter.

What does matter is what I know now beyond any shadow of a doubt: Jesus is real. That means He's alive. That's the big one!

JESUS. IS. REAL.

Are you ready to meet Him?
Are you ready?

"Moving Toward the Light"

Photo by Casey J. Cleveland

QUIET STRENGTH IN GOD

~ HE'S SO TOTALLY WORTH IT!

In 1956, Don Pike, my dad—he wasn't my dad yet because I wasn't born until 1973—bought a farm in Garrettsville, Ohio. Being a workaholic, he worked tenaciously for the next several years and built himself what I would consider a turkey farm empire! In every sense of the word, my dad was successful…yet unfulfilled. Dad knew he had every reason to be happy—he had a successful business, a lovely wife, five beautiful children, and influence throughout the community. Yet he knew he was miserable and didn't know why.

One night in 1972, both of my parents attended a revival service where Wade Clements preached a message of God's great love and His gift of eternal life through Jesus Christ. That night, my parents received the gift of God's love and asked Jesus to take over their lives, forgive them of their wrongdoings, and help them to be the people they were created to be.

Jesus changed them! My dad began to discover joy and fulfillment in his life like never before. My mom loved her family more deeply and trusted the Lord in everything.

When my mom discovered she was pregnant, she just knew I was a boy and would grow up to be a preacher. Obviously, this was before ultrasounds were available, so she was surprised to find out when I was born that I was a girl!

My parents and my whole family loved me well and taught me the ways of Jesus at a very early age. Not only did they teach me, but my parents lived the ways of Jesus in their everyday lives.

I was taught the value of God's Word, the Bible, and how it teaches us great wisdom for all areas of our lives. I watched my parents love each other well and learn to trust in the Lord for all things. I witnessed my mom and sister Cathy spending time in prayer and reading God's Word every morning.

When I was a little girl, I believed God loved me, so I received the gift of God's love and His invitation to become His child. At a young age, I grew to love God's Word by reading, learning, and leaning on its principles to guide my life.

Throughout the pages of this book, I have chronicled the journey of faith I have walked through various challenges and experiences. I am grateful I chose at a young age to receive God's gift of eternal life in Jesus, because now I want everyone I meet to know Jesus and how wonderful He is.

Following Jesus doesn't mean your life is going to be pain-free. My story alone is enough to demonstrate that. But following Jesus and trusting Him in the midst of our pain and confusion gives us comfort and help both in our times of need and in our times of joy.

I honestly do not know how I would have survived my life challenges if I had not chosen to follow Jesus. His Holy Spirit gave me the quiet strength needed to bring me through victoriously. Not every day feels like a victory, but I know He is with me, helps me, and loves me tremendously.

I believe if we truly begin to understand and grasp God's amazing, never-ending, boundless love for us, we will be drawn to love Him back. Consider these truths straight from the Bible:

> *And may you have the power to understand, as all God's people should, how wide, how long, how high, and how deep his love is. May you experience the love of Christ, though it is too great to understand fully. Then you will be made complete with all the fullness of life and power that comes from God. See how very much our Father loves us, for he*

calls us his children, and that is what we are! But the people who belong to this world don't recognize that we are God's children because they don't know him.

Despite all these things, overwhelming victory is ours through Christ, who loved us. And I am convinced that nothing can ever separate us from God's love. Neither death nor life, neither angels nor demons, neither our fears for today nor our worries about tomorrow—not even the powers of hell can separate us from God's love. No power in the sky above or in the earth below—indeed, nothing in all creation will ever be able to separate us from the love of God that is revealed in Christ Jesus our Lord (taken from Ephesians 3:18-19, I John 3:1, Romans 8:37-39 NLT).

God is so perfect and loves us so much, yet our wrongdoings keep us from truly connecting with him. That's why He sent Jesus—His perfect Son—to be born of a virgin, live a sinless life, die a gruesome death, and three days later be raised to life, overcoming the power of sin and death. After that, Jesus ascended to heaven, where He sits at the right hand of the throne of God. Yet He did not leave us alone or hopeless. He sent us His Spirit—the Holy Spirit—who empowers us to live the way God desires.

Because God loves you and me so much, He provided the way to Him through His Son Jesus. For Jesus said it Himself:

> *I am the way, the truth, and the life. No one can come to the Father except through me. (John 14:6 NLT).*

Some people may say that that statement sounds exclusive because it excludes other beliefs and religions. Yet consider this truth:

> *And everyone who calls on the name of the Lord will be saved (Acts 2:21).*

"Everyone" is inclusive. Anyone and everyone has the option to call on the name of the Lord, and everyone who does will be saved.

"What will everyone be saved from?" you might ask. We are saved from the punishment of our wrongdoing, which is spiritual death—forever separated from the God who loves you so much and provided a way for you to know Him.

To choose Jesus, all it takes to get started is a heartfelt prayer—a prayer that goes something like this:

> *"Jesus, I understand You are the way to God the Father who loves me extravagantly. Thank You for*

giving Your life for me. I ask You to forgive me of my wrongdoings, and I ask You to come in and help me to choose Your ways. Thank You for Your promise to be with me through my joys and my challenges. Thank You for Your gift of eternal life that I receive right now. I ask this in Your name, Jesus, Amen."

If you prayed that prayer in your heart, I have great news for you: you are forgiven and you are a new person because Jesus Christ has entered your life. That means you are different—not perfect, but changed.

In 2 Corinthians 5:17, the Bible says: "This means that anyone who belongs to Christ has become a new person. The old life is gone; a new life has begun!" (NLT). Isn't that great news?!

As a new person, we begin to think differently by soaking ourselves in the truth of God's Word. In the pages of the Bible, we discover who God is and how much He loves us. The Book of John in the New Testament is a great place to start reading.

Plugging yourself in to a Bible-teaching church is important to help you grow in your relationship with Jesus. A Bible study or a small group is a great way to become connected with other believers and to grow with Jesus.

Whatever it takes to get to know Jesus, I just want you to know He is so totally worth it!

Photo by Casey J. Cleveland

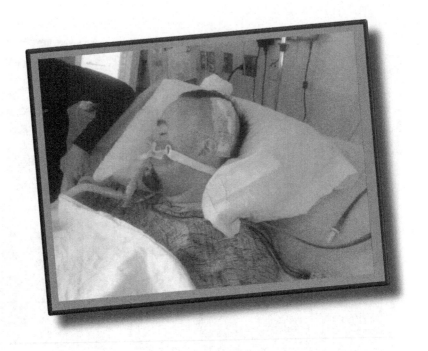

MONDAY, APRIL 21, 2014

<u>Miracle Man – Day 12</u>

The great BIG news for today is that Casey passed the barium swallow test and ate his first meal in 13 days!!! Yaaaaay! PTL! He spent most of the day awake and talking. I enjoyed some time alone with him this morning, and as I rested my head on the side of his bed, he very tenderly rubbed my back, just like before. (No apologies for the sappy details, Rhea.) :-) He is being very determined to get that right hand moving, and I saw big improvement today. At one point, he was resting his head on his left arm, so as he talked, he was moving his right arm very naturally. I think he's understanding us better, and he is starting to remember more people by name. He was talking about our oldest son by name today, as well as Rhea and Charles (our brother-in-law and business partner).

Prayer points:
- COMPLETE healing for Casey's brain, body, and soul
- that he continue to swallow all liquids and foods correctly into stomach, not lungs

• his blood pressure stay at a good rate, which will then allow him to be moved out of TICU into another room

• for The Lord to make it clear where Casey needs to go for rehab.

Again and again, thanks for the prayers. They're working so keep them up!!!!

Cindy, happily married to Casey

And if the Spirit of him who raised Jesus from the dead is living in you, he who raised Christ from the dead will also give life to your mortal bodies because of his Spirit who lives in you (Romans 8:11 NIV).

Miracle Man – Day 13
Journal entry by Gary Cleveland

Wow…After a difficult night, Casey was tired and not too happy this morning. But by lunchtime he was, with the help of his sister Rhea, able to eat his pureed lunch selections with Casey's great humor and tolerate his medicine sprinkled on top of pudding. Lunchtime today meant sitting in a chair to eat. After his lunch and several visitors, Casey was asked to try to stand up. So, with help, he was standing for the first time in two weeks. It appeared that the blood pressure was more under control today. The BP needs to stay under control for him to move out of the ICU and into a regular hospital room. So, overall another day of improvement for Casey.

Your prayers are so very much appreciated. We pray for continued strength for Casey and Cindy. For wisdom and compassion for the medical professionals. For God's guidance as we look forward to rehab. For healing in Casey's mind to help his speech and memory.

Our family has been honored and humbled by expressions of love from our community of believers. For those in the Lakeland area, save this Saturday evening for the benefit concert at Shepherd's Community United Methodist.

While I don't know exactly how we will get there, I only know that God has great things planned for Casey. Thanks for joining us on this journey.

BLESS (AFFECTIONATELY, GRATEFULLY PRAISE) THE LORD, O MY SOUL, AND FORGET NOT [ONE OF] ALL HIS BENEFITS—WHO FORGIVES [EVERY ONE OF] ALL YOUR INIQUITIES, WHO HEALS [EACH ONE OF] ALL YOUR DISEASES (PSALM 103:2-3 AMPC).

<u>Miracle Man – Day 14</u>

Casey's miracles today include standing up with the help of the PT and nurse, and taking tiny steps as he turned to sit in a chair. He was able to follow most of the Physical Therapist's instructions, and she was very pleased with his progress. He was also feeding himself today with his left hand!

I'm working on the song "Oceans" to sing at the Night of Worship benefit concert this Saturday night, so we had the song playing in the room today. Casey was clearly remembering the melody, even though the words weren't all coming out right, yet. He would close his eyes as he concentrated on the words, and then he'd start praying, "Bring them to the front, Lord...Yes...This is good..." We even had a few moments as a duet, and I was loving that!

He's been off the blood pressure drip and onto oral meds, and his levels have been good. Which gives us great hope that he will reach another milestone tomorrow—moving out of Trauma ICU and into a room upstairs! More details on that tomorrow...

Specific prayers:
• COMPLETE healing for Casey's brain, body, and soul
• Wisdom for all those caring for Casey

- Easy transition upstairs
- Vision be perfect
- Blood pressure remain at good numbers
- And in Casey's words, "Bring them to the front, Lord!" Bring the words he's trying to say, so he can communicate effectively and perfectly, as well as understand correctly.

Today is the two week mark! Just think, two weeks ago, we were told Casey may be paralyzed from the neck down, and that he wouldn't understand or be able to communicate. Well, God has "flipped" all of those predictions and performed miracle after miracle! In many ways, these have been the longest 2 weeks of my life, but at the same time, I'm so excited about what God is doing and how He is going to use Casey's life to do more miracles! GOD IS SO GOOD!!!

Keep the prayers going, and come enjoy God's presence with music at the Night of Worship Benefit Concert this Saturday night, 7:00 p.m., at Shepherd's Community UMC, 2165 Shepherd Road, Lakeland Florida 33811

Cindy, happily married to Casey

P.S. Here are a few of God's promises that have sustained me the past 2 weeks...

Then they cried to the Lord in their trouble, and he saved them from their distress. He sent out his word and healed them; he rescued them from the grave. Let them give thanks to the Lord for his unfailing love and his wonderful deeds for mankind. Let them sacrifice thank offerings and tell of his works with songs of joy (Psalm 107:19-22 NIV).

I remain confident of this: I will see the goodness of the Lord in the land of the living. Wait for the Lord; be strong and take heart and wait for the Lord (Psalm 27:13, 14 NIV).

Surely he took up our pain and bore our suffering, yet we considered him punished by God, stricken by him, and afflicted. But he was pierced for our transgressions, he was crushed for our iniquities; the punishment that brought us peace was on him, and by his wounds we are healed. We all, like sheep, have gone astray, each of us has turned to our own way; and the Lord has laid on him the iniquity of us all (Isaiah 53:4-6 NIV).

"He himself bore our sins" in his body on the cross, so that we might die to sins and live for righteousness; "by his wounds you have been healed" (1 Peter 2:24 NIV).

And if the Spirit of him who raised Jesus from the dead is living in you, he who raised Christ from the dead will also give life to your mortal bodies because of his Spirit who lives in you (Romans 8:11 NIV).

<u>Miracle Man – Day 15</u>
Journal entry by Gary Cleveland

Casey's day 15 brought both elation and concern. What a ride we are on! Every day is an adventure.

Elation...
1. His progress has been so dramatic that the doctor released him from ICU to a regular hospital room!!!
2. He was allowed to eat regular food!!!
3. There are no IVs or cath in him any longer!!!

Concern...Because of his newfound freedom, he needs to understand how to push the button for the nurse. But I'm not sure he has that understanding. Walking to the restroom requires a lot of effort on his part and two caregivers. His ticket out of the hospital will be punched if he can pass the "walk to the bathroom test."

On the lighter side, Rhea and I gave him a haircut tonight. His new 'do is a very sporty buzz cut number 2. Now his left side surgical haircut has got company with the right side. Cindy says he looks sexy.

My prayer points are:
1. Please pray for full restoration of use of arms,

legs, speech and mind.

2. Pray for the medical staff and doctors of Lakeland Regional Medical Center. For wisdom and compassion to surround Casey.

3. Pray for wisdom for his family to know the Lord's leading in finding the right rehab facility.

4. Please pray that Casey's wife and sons remain healthy, strong, and comforted.

Praise to the lover of our soul.

FRIDAY, APRIL 25, 2014

Miracle Man – Day 16

Casey experienced a couple ups and downs today, but overall, still a good day. When I arrived this morning, the PT, OT, and nurse were working with him. As soon as I walked in, they were amazed at how much better he started communicating. You see, Casey is currently experiencing "expressive aphasia," which basically means he knows what he wants to say, but he's having trouble finding the right words. As you can imagine, this can get very frustrating, and today was one of those frustrating days for him.

On the "up" side, during his PT/OT session, he was able to walk to the bathroom (with much help) and brush his teeth! After fighting off a low-grade fever and overall not feeling well today, he ended the day in good spirits and feeling much better.

He seems to be understanding us better every day. In fact, tonight I told him about the Caring Bridge updates and how we're titling them "Miracle Man." He seemed to like that! And when I told him there were over 3,000 times people have visited our update pages, he was very impressed and answered, "Wow!"

In the event that any of you may be concerned about Casey's wellbeing now that he's been moved to a regular room with less supervision, rest assured that we worked on some new arrangements today, including that fact that I am here with Casey now, spending the night. Please pray we both sleep well. :)

Let's thank God in advance for these things, as if they're already accomplished:

> • the connections in his brain work correctly so he can say what he wants to say, and so he can see correctly, and so he can continue moving and feeling his right side.
> • COMPLETE healing for Casey's brain, body, and soul.
> • protection for any infections, etc.
> • wisdom be given to those caring for him, and for his family as we choose a rehab facil-

ity very soon.

• continued good health and strength for the whole family as we care for Casey, too.

• that lives will be touched and people will be changed at the Night of Worship benefit concert tomorrow (Saturday) night, led by LivingSong, at Shepherd's Community UMC, 2165 Shepherd Road, Lakeland, 33811. Hope you can come, 7:00 p.m.

Good night, Cindy, happily married to Casey

SATURDAY, APRIL 26, 2014

Miracle Man – Day 17

Today started out with some surprising news. After the okay from the neurosurgeon, Casey could be discharged from the hospital as early as today! Well, since there are still logistics to work out concerning the rehab center, he was not discharged today, but quite possibly on Monday. :)

All four of our boys made a visit to see Daddy today. Casey definitely remembers his boys and often sheds a tear when he talks about or sees them. Our oldest, Solomon (age 8), decided he wanted to stay with Daddy today, so Solomon and I spent the rest of our day with Casey. Solomon was such a good helper during lunch by helping his daddy eat.

Tonight's benefit concert was so rewarding in so many ways! Thanks to all of you that attended. Thanks to all who gave so generously. Thanks to all the lead worshipers and musicians, servers, greeters, raffle givers, etc. It was an amazing and successful night all the way around! And BEST of all, six people prayed to receive Jesus as Savior tonight!!! God is so good! He's continuing to work good all around us and through us!

One last thing before I fall asleep…I talked to one of the TICU nurses tonight and asked her about what she would say about Casey's progress. She said, "In the ICU, we see many people come in with trauma injuries like Casey's. But how he has progressed is 'way beyond science.' Yes, he's young, and yes, he has a great support system of family, friends, and faith, but the rate at which he has progressed is beyond anything that could be explained in the medical field." God is working a MIRACLE in Miracle Man. Keep up the prayers!!!!

Goodnight,
Cindy, happily married to Miracle Man

Bless (affectionately, gratefully praise) the Lord, O my soul, and forget not [one of] all His benefits— Who forgives [every one of] all your iniquities, Who heals [each one of] all your diseases (Psalm 103:2-3 AMPC).

Miracle Man – Day 18

We continue to give thanks to God for Casey's improvements every day! On this Sunday, Casey and Gary (his dad) enjoyed their own church service together while listening to the live stream contemporary service at First United Methodist Church. All four of our boys enjoyed time with Daddy today, as well as our pastor and several friends. Casey's communication is definitely improving. Four days ago, Casey talked very intentionally with Pastor Mark about an incident that Casey experienced, and we think it was not long after he had the stroke. Today, Casey talked about the same experience, and although we're still piecing it all together, his communication was much better. We pray he continues to remember what happened, even after he can put all the proper words together.

Our prayers remain steadfast:
• the connections in his brain work correctly so he can say what he wants to say, and so he can see correctly, and so he can continue moving and feeling his right side.
• COMPLETE healing for Casey's brain, body, and soul.
• protection for any infections, etc.

• wisdom be given to those caring for him, and for his family as we choose a rehab facility very soon.

• continued good health and strength for the whole family as we care for Casey, too.

Goodnight,
Cindy, happily married to Casey

Bless (affectionately, gratefully praise) the Lord, O my soul, and forget not [one of] all His benefits— Who forgives [every one of] all your iniquities, Who heals [each one of] all your diseases. (Psalm 103:2-3 AMPC).

MONDAY, APRIL 28, 2014

Miracle Man – Day 19

The highlight of today is Casey has moved out of Lakeland's hospital! This afternoon he was transferred to Joy-Fuller Rehabilitation Center in Winter Haven's hospital. My heart is overjoyed to be moving on to the next big step on this journey. On the drive over to Winter Haven, I kept praying, "Thank You, Lord! Thank You for hearing the prayers of Your people. Thank You for getting us this far..." Even with a heart filled with gratitude, it was difficult to leave Casey there tonight. New environment, new staff, lots of questions, etc. I know Casey is ready to improve, but today he was definitely discouraged, especially in regards to the expressive aphasia. He wants the words to come, so I keep reminding him that he's improving every day.

Please pray:
• for Casey as he starts speech, occupational, and physical therapies tomorrow.
• for wisdom and understanding for nurses, therapists, doctors, etc. assisting him.
• for COMPLETE healing of his brain, body, and soul.
• for the words to come and his vision to clear up so he can see perfectly.
• that the staff will enjoy working with him and that God will be glorified in all things.

Thanks for all your prayers. Thanks for all your giving. Thanks for being Casey's Army of God!

Goodnight!

Cindy, happily married to Casey

You will keep in perfect peace those whose minds are steadfast, because they trust in you. Trust in the Lord forever, for the Lord, the Lord himself, is the Rock eternal (Isaiah 26:3-4 NIV).

Miracle Man – Day 20

Casey had a great first day at rehab. They kept him VERY busy with speech, physical, and occupational therapies, throw in a recreational therapy, two neuro-psychology sessions, and a swallow test, plus visits from our boys, other family, and friends. That was Casey's day! I'm certain he's thrilled to be physically doing something toward improving, instead of lying around in a hospital bed.

From my heart to yours, it's tough to see him work so hard just to stand up, knowing that three weeks ago, he was climbing a 12-foot ladder. I'm confident—even in what I don't see yet—that Casey will be doing all his normal activities and then some, for God is raising him up and completing the good work He has started in Casey!

Please pray:
• for Casey as he continues speech, occupational, and physical therapies tomorrow.
• for wisdom and supernatural understanding for the nurses, therapists, doctors, etc. assisting him.
• for COMPLETE healing of his brain, body, and soul.
• for the words to come and his vision to

clear up so he can see perfectly.

• that the staff will enjoy working with him and that God will be glorified in all things.

Until next time, keep believing, keep praying, keep trusting…

Good night!

Cindy, happily married to Casey

I LOVE YOU, LORD,

MY STRENGTH

(PSALM 18:1 NIV).

<u>Miracle Man – Day 21</u>

Casey's second day at rehab had some highlights:

• He walked up steps, walked down the hall, and walked for the first time without a walker!

• He played UNO and beat the two therapists in the first two games! (I don't suppose it's worth mentioning that when I joined them in the third game, I beat them all…no it's probably not worth mentioning that…heehee!)

• He took a shower! :-)

I met with the neuropsychologist today. He mentioned that Casey is going to be a delight for the team to work with because of his good attitude and determination. He mentioned that the aphasia is pretty severe and Casey does a better job understanding when he can see a picture or an action. We also have a better understanding of Casey's current visual challenges. In physical therapy, his balance was better today than yesterday, and I was so excited to see him walking without a walker but only with the support of the PT.

Prayers continue:

• Let's agree that the neurological pathways, particularly those involving his understanding and his words, would be reconnected and/or that new and better ones would be found.

• Let's agree that Casey's vision be corrected completely.

• Let's agree that the right side of his body continue to regain its feeling and movement.

• Let's agree for supernatural wisdom to be given to the staff and supernatural favor be upon Casey as they discuss his goals, plan of action, and length of stay in a meeting tomorrow morning from 10:45-12:00.

• Let's agree for Casey's COMPLETE healing of his brain, body, and soul.

Thanks for standing with us, reading these updates, praying, believing, and trusting. I just have to believe...

Goodnight!

Cindy, happily married to Miracle Man

<u>Miracle Man – Day 22</u>

When I arrived this morning, Casey was playing UNO and then Dominos. He does a good job understanding the concepts of the games, but his vision is currently giving him limitations. One of the major highlights of today was watching Casey walk down the hall without a walker, only a gate belt and a PT assisting! Pastor Mark and Emma were his audience during his walk this morning, then Casey's parents and our two older boys were there for his afternoon walk, which brought tears to Mom's and Dad's eyes. (A video has been posted on my Facebook page.)

The speech therapist told me that Casey did much better today than she expected. He worked very hard at trying to get the right sounds out. Sometimes he said the words perfectly and other times he came close. She explained that with aphasia the words are in the brain; it's just accessing them when you want them. So, although Casey is talking a lot, he's not always saying the words he wants to say. And, like today, just repeating a name after me was challenging, or in Casey's words, "It's so weird!"

So, now for the "sappy" news…While I sat with Casey at lunch, he looked at me and said, "I love you." I told him, "I love you, too, Babe." Then his eyes started filling up with tears, and he said, "I don't know why

I'm getting so emotional over this." He found all the right words—it was a beautiful moment!

Please pray:
• that Casey's brain would make new and better pathways, particularly in regards to his speech/understanding/reading/writing (they'll all related), and his vision.
• that his body continue to be strengthened and that his right side get all its feeling back.
• for COMPLETE healing for Casey's brain, body, and soul.
• for Casey's body to respond well to the medications.
• for wisdom to be given to the doctors, nurses, therapists, and staff as they care for Casey.

Thank you, Casey's Army

of God! We couldn't do this without you!!!

Goodnight...

Cindy, happily married to the man of my dreams!

<u>Miracle Man – Day 23</u>

Remember back on Day 7 when Casey pulled the ventilator out of his mouth at the brief moment when the nurse stepped out of the room…and then on Day 8 when he pulled the feeding tube out of his nose after removing the padded mitt from his hand??? Well, this morning he pulled another sneaky moment on us. As soon as the night-shift "sitter" left the room at 7:00 a.m., Casey decided he would get out of bed and walk to the bathroom on his own, and that's exactly where the nurse found him! Thank God for his angels stationed around him, protecting him from falling! He was reprimanded for his actions, but quite frankly, I don't think he's a bit remorseful!!! As I keep saying, keep the prayers going—they're working! :-)

I posted a video on my FB page of Casey kicking a small soccer ball in PT today, and I am reminded that three weeks ago, he was on life-support. We serve a mighty, mighty God!

In speech therapy today, he did such a great job repeating the sounds the therapist was saying while looking at her and himself in a mirror. With years of vocal training, Casey is very accustomed to watching himself in the mirror as he develops the sounds he wants. We also continued to work on names in our family, as well as identifying objects on a table.

And now it's time for the "sappy" lunchtime update...So we were talking during lunch about our boys, and what they're doing, and who they're with today, etc. Again, he started tearing up because he so wants to be the daddy our boys need. Then he proceeded to tell me how "awesome" he thinks I am! :-) Gotta love this guy!

Please pray:

• that Casey be protected from any harm and from falling, especially if he tries another one of his stunts.

• for Casey's COMPLETE healing on his brain, body, and soul.

• for the proper connections to be made in his brain so he can speak/understand-/write/read correctly, and so he can see perfectly.

• for me and the boys...peace, strength, health, protection, and anything else God brings to your mind...

• for Stella (whom I met today) and her husband who is battling lung cancer.

Thanks for praying, believing, fighting, and watching God unfold this miracle before our eyes. Thank you Lord, and thank you, Casey's Army of God!

Good night!

Cindy, happily married to Miracle Man

BECAUSE YOUR LOVE IS BETTER THAN LIFE, MY LIPS WILL GLORIFY YOU. I WILL PRAISE YOU AS LONG AS I LIVE, AND IN YOUR NAME I WILL LIFT UP MY HANDS. I WILL BE FULLY SATISFIED AS WITH THE RICHEST OF FOODS; WITH SINGING LIPS MY MOUTH WILL PRAISE YOU (PSALM 63:3-5 NIV).

<u>Miracle Man – Day 24</u>

Casey had another full day of rehab today, and he did great! Tears came again today, but not because of a "sappy" moment. No, it was because I showed him a calendar. I showed him today's date and his projected departure day, and that made him cry. He's ready to be out of there and back to real life. Patient endurance—that's what we're developing—patient endurance...

Rhea worked with him this evening on speech, and when she sang the syllables, he did very well. Casey's singing talent will come in handy these days!

Thanks for continuing the prayers:
- Casey's COMPLETE healing on brain, body, and soul.
- Protection, good health, strength, peace—for Casey and ALL the family.
- VISION and SPEECH—pray for all the right connections be made in his brain.
- Wisdom for doctors, nurses, therapists, sitters, family
- Pray that I develop better time-management skills, so I can start getting to bed before midnight...(And for those of you that have told me you wait up for these updates to post, you'll be grateful for the answer to this prayer, too. LOL!)

The thief comes only in order to steal and kill and destroy. I came that they may have and enjoy life, and have it in abundance (to the full, till it overflows) (John 10:10 AMP).

SUNDAY, MAY 4, 2014

<u>Miracle Man – Day 25</u>

In an effort to go to bed before midnight, I will attempt to make this brief....

Casey had another full day of therapy, and Gary spent most of the day with him. Sounds to me like PT and OT went well. Speech therapy had its challenges today, but tomorrow is another day.

Casey and Gary watched part of the church service at FUMC online and saw Pastor David McEntire talk about Casey's prayer quilt. Thanks to all of you who participated in that! Then they watched part of a message from Pastor Mark Reynolds at Shepherd's Community UMC titled "What Would Casey Say." Apparently, Casey and his dad shed a few tears as they listened to Mark discuss the first few hours of Casey's stroke journey. Sounds like the rest of the message (based on Ephesians 6) will have to be watched another time...

212

The boys and I and our marvelous babysitter visited Daddy at dinner time. It's always such a delight to see Casey interact with his little loves. :-)

Three dear friends visited today that hadn't seen Casey since last Sunday. They all commented on how much Casey has improved in one week, especially in his communication. Thank You, Lord!

Let's expect great strides this week, especially in regards to his speech/understanding/writing/reading, and in regards to his vision—for the proper connections to be made. Thanks for the continued prayers for us ALL!

Good night! (earlier than most nights!) :-)

Cindy, happily married to Casey

Let everything that has breath and every breath of life praise the Lord! Praise the Lord! (Hallelujah!) (Psalm 150:6 AMP).

<u>Miracle Man – Day 26</u>

Casey's morning was less than ideal. He was tired, partially due to his not sleeping well last night. He's not a morning person anyway, and I'm fairly convinced that the medications he takes in the morning make him drowsy. Headaches are often a factor in the morning, but he seems to feel great by the afternoon.

So, his afternoon speech therapy session went very well. Sometimes, due to the aphasia, it's difficult to know what Casey understands, so I was very encouraged today to see that he can still read words. On a flipbook, he had a picture and then three words to choose from, and most of the time, he chose the correct word! Yaaaay! Praise the Lord!

In PT, he did a great job walking, moving along fairly fast today. He did some "step aerobics," an obstacle course, and various arm and leg exercises that also strengthen his core.

In pictures or videos, you may notice a patch on his glasses. Due to the vision challenges he has currently, the patch is switched every hour, in order to strengthen both eyes individually. He was asking me today if his vision would always be like it is now. I told him it will continue to improve and that we are believing for his TOTAL healing.

So, please pray:

• for his vision to be completely restored—no blind spots or double vision.

• for his brain to make all the right proper connections.

• for Casey's COMPLETE healing of his brain, body, and soul.

• that the CAT scan he had today would be another good report.

• for continued strength, wisdom, peace, and provision for myself and the boys and for all the staff attending to Casey.

• that Casey sleep well tonight.

Goodnight All!

O COME, let us sing to the Lord; let us make a joyful noise to the Rock of our salvation! Let us come before His presence with thanksgiving; let us make a joyful noise to Him with songs of praise! For the Lord is a great God, and a great King above all gods. O come, let us worship and bow down, let us kneel before the Lord our Maker [in reverent praise and supplication] (Psalm 95:1-3, 6 AMP).

Miracle Man – Day 27

I just posted three videos on Facebook that I think best describe today. (If you're on FB, send me a friend request so you can see for yourselves.) If you're not on FB, I'll give you a quick description of the videos:

Video 1 – Casey walking, quite quickly, down the hall with the physical therapist only steadying his shoulders to be sure he doesn't lose his balance.

Video 2 – A sample of his speech therapy session today. He's repeating what the pathologist was saying while looking at her and himself in the mirror. Although the words and sounds are in his brain, the challenge at times is accessing the words when he wants them. He did very well with this today!

Video 3 – Our two oldest boys coming to visit Daddy. It was a sweet reunion! :-)

As a whole today, Casey did very well. He slept well last night, rested well today, didn't eat well but after a snack he felt much better. He enjoyed visits from close family and friends, all of which were impressed with his increasing ability to communicate.

That being said, please continue to pray:
• for a good night sleep for him.
• for COMPLETE healing of Casey's brain, body, and soul.
• for all the right connections to be made in his brain, especially in regards to his VISION and COMMUNICATION.
• for God to continue to perform miracles in our Miracle Man.

4:30 in the morning marks the start of this adventure 4 weeks ago. Each Wednesday morning since then, I've been awake around 4:30 a.m. (We'll see if I get the luxury of being awakened again tonight...) During those moments of the unknown in the early hours on April 9, I listened to the song "Your Grace Finds Me" written by Matt Redman and Jonas Myrin. It's a beautiful song with powerful lyrics.

<u>Miracle Man – Day 29</u>

The highlight of the day was handing Casey his guitar and watching him make beautiful music! Thank You, Lord!!! Check out the video on mine or Gary's FB page...it's good stuff and has already brought several to tears.

Casey also walked down the hall today without the PT touching him!!! That was great to see!

Playing guitar and walking—those are 2 biggies, so keep the prayers going, especially for Casey's COMPLETE healing of his brain, body, and soul!

Gotta go to sleep...Good night!

I've had these verses on my refrigerator for months:

> *Your righteousness also, O God, is very high [reaching to the heavens], You Who have done great things; O God, who is like You, or who is Your equal? You Who have shown us [all] troubles great and sore will quicken us again and will bring us up again from the depths of the earth. Increase my greatness (my honor) and turn and comfort me (Psalm 71:19-21 AMP).*

Miracle Man – Day 30

One month ago today our lives were forever changed. And I have a feeling it's not just our family, for many of you have said your faith has been strengthened or you have been inspired through this journey. I know my faith will never be the same. I know I will never be the same person I was before April 9.

As many of you know, four and a half years ago, Casey and I experienced the pain of the death of our only daughter, Selah. Then, three years ago, my sister Cathy joined her in heaven. Neither of these ended the way we wanted them to end, nor the way we had prayed and believed. We could have given up all hope in God at those times. We could have looked at those situations and come to the conclusion that God doesn't answer prayers anymore. But Casey and I made the choice to keep believing and trusting God…to keep standing on His Word and believing His promises…to keep giving God praise for He is still worthy!

And I'm so glad we did keep believing, and for ALL of you that have prayed and believed with us, we are seeing God answering our prayers! The rate at which Casey is progressing is nothing short of a modern-day miracle! This is beyond science…a.k.a. "Supernatural."

So, the good reports continue today…Casey

walked outside today! And he did great! More progress was made in speech therapy today. Pastor Mark visited Casey, and as Casey talked about events, he spoke with very little difficulty.

Please continue all the prayers:
• COMPLETE healing for Casey's brain, body, and soul.
• It should be a fairly relaxing weekend for him, so pray he gets the rest he needs for another big week ahead.
• Continued wisdom for all those attending to him.
• Wisdom for me and all the family.
• Strength for me and the boys. It's been a month without their daddy around and we all get weary at times...
• Pray that Casey never loses his focus and never doubts the good plans God has for him.

In closing, please accept the sincere and enormous amount of gratitude that Casey and I and all our family feel toward all of you who have given so generously. Financial gifts. Gift cards. Meals. Boy-sitting. All kinds and every gift. Groceries. Prayers. And so, so much more...I wish I could write each of you a "thank you" card, but there's way too many of you to thank! I wish we could take each and every one of you out to dinner, so why don't we plan on this: when Casey is all better, we'll plan a worship night with food for all! Sound good?!?!

With prayers for all of you reading this...Good night!

> *For I know the thoughts and plans that I have for you, says the Lord, thoughts and plans for welfare and peace and not for evil, to give you hope in your final outcome (Jeremiah 29:11 AMP).*

SATURDAY, MAY 10, 2014

Miracle Man – Day 31

Casey had no therapy sessions today, so the morning was filled with much-needed rest and the afternoon was filled with visits from family and a very special friend. Stanley George has been a good friend of ours for years and is a very talented musician and worship leader. He flew down from New York so he could visit Casey, and what a great time we had! I posted a video on FB of our "music therapy" session in the lobby of the hospital. In the video, you can tell that Casey hears the melody and rhythm very well. The words don't come quickly enough for him to sing them all yet, but he was getting a few of the sounds out which is marvelous!

Apparently, he enjoyed some more laughs and video-making this evening with his crazy sister Rhea. Their Mother's Day video to their mom, Tee Cleveland, is quite humorous!

Thanks for the continued prayers, especially for Casey's COMPLETE healing of his brain, body, and soul.

Good night!

And if the Spirit of Him Who raised up Jesus from the dead dwells in you, [then] He Who raised up Christ Jesus from the dead will also restore to life your mortal (short-lived, perishable) bodies through His Spirit Who dwells in you (Romans 8:11 AMP).

<u>Miracle Man – Day 32</u>

Casey's day was filled with family fun! His dad joined him in the morning, and they enjoyed their own church service together. Mother's Day lunch was provided by Boston Market and brought in with Casey's mom, sister, and grandmother. Casey enjoyed a little rest before a short PT session. Then our four boys and I, along with my parents, provided an hour-and-a-half of entertainment and chaos! I posted a video on FB with a snippet of our fun… :-)

Casey has another full week of therapies and miracles ahead of him. Please pray for the following:

- COMPLETE healing for Casey's brain, body, and soul.
- that Casey would remain strong and encouraged.
- that Casey's vision and communication be complete restored!
- Wisdom for doctors, nurses, therapists, etc.
- Wisdom for us as we make plans for his return home, i.e. outpatient therapy facility, needs for Casey's care at home, etc.

I'm not sure I should admit this publicly, but today was the first time I ever got on the donation site that sweet people from our church set up for our family.

I have been overwhelmed and humbled by the response of so many caring people that have given so generously out of the kindness of their hearts. If you're one of those kind people, THANK YOU from the bottom of my heart!!! So many people have given so generously, and some of them we've never met before! God is so good, and His people are, too!

Happy Mother's Day – God Bless – Good night!

When I said, "My foot is slipping," your unfailing love, Lord, supported me. When anxiety was great within me, your consolation brought me joy (Psalm 94:18, 19 NIV).

<u>Miracle Man – Day 33</u>

Casey had another good day. I enjoyed time with him this evening as we watched the video of our crazy boys during yesterday's visit! We laughed and talked, and as we talked about what our lives look like now, he spoke briefly about the stroke. I wish I was recording some of the things he said, but one that stands out to me was when he said he lay there and prayed, "God, I love You." Through all of this, Casey has not stopped counting his blessings. On several occasions, I've heard him randomly say, "Thank You, Lord." He's giving God praise "...in all circumstances."

Please pray for:
• Casey's COMPLETE healing of his brain, body, and soul.
• Wisdom, protection, and good health.

Thanks for all the prayers, love, and support!

Good night…

Rejoice always, pray continually, give thanks in all circumstances; for this is God's will for you in Christ Jesus (1 Thessalonians 5:16-18 NIV).

<u>Miracle Man – Day 34</u>

Today I took our oldest boy with me so Solomon could spend the day with Daddy. In PT, he helped pass the ball to Casey, and Casey dribbled the ball down the hallway. I took a walk with Casey, while the PT instructed me on how to help and support Casey. We also watched a speech/recreational therapy session involving a game with numbers. Casey did well.

Casey decided to try his eyes without a patch today. Individually, he can see fine out of each eye, but when they're working together, apparently it's double or triple vision, with stationary objects that seem to be moving. We're trying to explain to him that his eyes have to learn how to work together again, but as you can imagine, he can get very frustrated with the vision challenges.

So, the biggie prayers would be:
• Casey's vision – eyes work good together, and brain figure out how to make that happen.
• Casey's communication—understanding/speech/reading/writing—brain make the connections and heal completely so Casey can communicate clearly.
• COMPLETE healing for Casey's brain,

body, and soul.
• Wisdom and protection for all.

Thanks again for ALL you do to love and support us all at this time...

Good night!

Humble yourselves, therefore, under God's mighty hand, that he may lift you up in due time. Cast all your anxiety on him because he cares for you (1 Peter 5:6, 7 NIV).

<u>Miracle Man – Day 35</u>

Today was Isaac's (boy #2) special day with Daddy. :-) When we got to the rehab center, it was Daddy's "rest" time, so all three of us snuggled up on his bed and watched Isaac play Angry Birds GO! on Daddy's iPad. Sweet times...

I was not in his morning PT session, but I was told he was having a great deal of fun with the soccer ball. Rather than returning the ball back to the PT assistant, he was kicking it so hard that the assistant was having to play dodge ball! In the afternoon session, we walked outside. He did well, although something made him feel "weird," so after a few minutes, we returned to the inside.

In Occupational Therapy, he played his guitar! Because the right side has less feeling right now, it's hard for him to hold a guitar pick. He did eventually try it though.

I was not in either Speech Therapy session, but I was told he was working on spelling words with the use of some apps on the iPad.

Please pray:
• that Casey gets a good night's sleep...it does his body good.
• that whatever was affecting him outside to-

day would no longer be an issue.

• 3 biggies—vision, communication, balance.

• COMPLETE healing of Casey's brain, body, and soul.

Sweet dreams…Good night!

But he said to me, "My grace is sufficient for you, for my power is made perfect in weakness." Therefore I will boast all the more gladly about my weaknesses, so that Christ's power may rest on me. That is why, for Christ's sake, I delight in weaknesses, in insults, in hardships, in persecutions, in difficulties. For when I am weak, then I am strong (2 Corinthians 12:9, 10 NIV).

THURSDAY, MAY 15, 2014

Miracle Man – Day 36

Casey had a very full schedule today, and he did great! His morning was filled with therapies and a visit from Pastor Mark Reynolds. Mark said that Casey spoke very fluently during their thirty minutes together and hardly stumbled over his words. With Mark, Casey often speaks about what he experienced either during or shortly after his stroke. Casey is very aware that God is up to something, and it's big! He told Mark that this is not the end, but only the beginning. Although he is certainly aware that he cannot see well or talk very well right now, yet he declares boldly, "It is not over!"

During my time with him, we talked together, rested together, and danced together. It was a good day! :-)

In PT, he did "step aerobics," but this time, the step was lifted two notches higher than last time.

His dad and sister visited with him this evening. They made crazy videos together. It's so great to see him laugh and to see his personality come out!

Prayers:
• Pray that we learn to manage his surroundings so he is not overstimulated.
• Pray he sleeps well tonight.
• Pray for his vision and communication to continue to improve.
• Pray for COMPLETE healing of Casey's brain, body, and soul.

Thanks for ALL the prayers! They're working, so keep them up!

And we know that in all things God works for the good of those who love him, who have been called according to his purpose (Romans 8:28 NIV).

Miracle Man – Day 37

We give thanks for another great day! In Speech Therapy, Casey was writing words correctly—on his own—using his right hand! That's huge! He's still needing a "prompt" to say the word correctly, but that will come. Keep praying for this! In Occupational Therapy, he had a couple different activities that exercised the right hand, so his right hand worked hard today.

In Physical Therapy, he walked outside again and today all was well. She also had a few pictures of items he was supposed to find in the gift shop. He found a couple of them, which was good, especially considering his vision gives him additional challenges these days.

He met with the neuropsychologist about his vision. I did not get the report, but according to Casey, someone has "finally" figured out how Casey is seeing. I look forward to hearing what else we can do to help improve his vision. Keep the prayers going!

Please pray for:

• Vision completely restored soon.

• Continued improvement on speaking, understanding, reading, and writing.

• Continued development and strength in his right side.

• COMPLETE healing in Casey's brain, body, and soul.

• Wisdom for all attending to Casey's care, and wisdom as we make arrangements for his return home.

You cannot be thanked enough for all your prayers, love and support for our family! You are treasured! Sweet dreams...

So God has given both his promise and his oath. These two things are unchangeable because it is impossible for God to lie. Therefore, we who have fled to him for refuge can have great confidence as we hold to the hope that lies before us. This hope is a strong and trustworthy anchor for our souls. It leads us through the curtain into God's inner sanctuary. Jesus has already gone in there for us. He has become our eternal High Priest in the order of Melchizedek (Hebrews 6:18-20 NLT).

<u>Miracle Man – Day 38</u>

Gotta make this short—morning will be here soon…

Today our oldest son, Solomon, enjoyed his special time with Daddy. We brought him one of his favorite breakfast items—apple fritter from Hole in One Donuts. Yum! Yum! You can watch a video of him on FB have lots of fun with his fritter! :-)

He only had a speech session today, where he worked on writing and saying the names of our boys. Other than that, he "rested" today, which included some time sitting outside enjoying our beautiful weather, and the daily visit from his sister Rhea.

Keep the prayers going; they're working. More miracles planned for tomorrow!!!

"Have faith in God," Jesus answered. "Truly I tell you, if anyone says to this mountain, 'Go, throw yourself into the sea,' and does not doubt in their heart but believes that what they say will happen, it will be done for them. Therefore I tell you, whatever you ask for in prayer, believe that you have received it, and it will be yours. And when you stand praying, if you hold anything against anyone, forgive them, so that your Father in heaven may forgive you your sins" (Mark 11:22-25 NIV).

I LOVE YOU, LORD, MY STRENGTH. THE LORD IS MY ROCK, MY FORTRESS

AND MY DELIVERER; MY GOD IS MY ROCK, IN WHOM I TAKE REFUGE,

MY SHIELD AND THE HORN OF MY SALVATION, MY STRONGHOLD.

I CALLED TO THE LORD, WHO IS WORTHY OF PRAISE, AND I HAVE BEEN

SAVED FROM MY ENEMIES. THE CORDS OF DEATH ENTANGLED ME;

THE TORRENTS OF DESTRUCTION OVERWHELMED ME. THE CORDS OF

THE GRAVE COILED AROUND ME; THE SNARES OF DEATH CONFRONTED

ME. IN MY DISTRESS I CALLED TO THE LORD; I CRIED TO MY GOD FOR

HELP. FROM HIS TEMPLE HE HEARD MY VOICE; MY CRY CAME BEFORE

HIM, INTO HIS EARS

(PSALM 18:1-6 NIV).

"...NO WEAPON FORGED AGAINST YOU WILL PREVAIL,

AND YOU WILL REFUTE EVERY TONGUE THAT ACCUSES YOU.

THIS IS THE HERITAGE OF THE SERVANTS OF THE LORD, AND THIS IS

THEIR VINDICATION FROM ME," DECLARES THE LORD

(ISAIAH 54:17 NIV).

234

<u>Miracle Man – Day 39</u>

This morning Casey watched our church service "live stream" across the internet! One of the reasons that's worth mentioning is because streaming live was a vision of Casey's, and the amazing team of people at Shepherd's Community UMC in Lakeland, Florida, made it happen! Hallelujah! (Check us out live on Sunday mornings or anytime at www.scumc.net – that's my commercial! :-))

Casey had a restful day, until I brought all four boys over at dinner time. Then it got wild and crazy!!! But we had a good visit with Daddy and his interaction with the boys was very pleasant. A cute video of him playing with our youngest is on Facebook. Sweet times...

Casey was struggling to see well out of his right eye, and he seemed to have less feeling in his right side. So please pray...

Prayers:
• right eye and feeling in right side be COMPLETELY restored.
• strength and good health as he has his last few days of therapy there.
• COMPLETE healing of Casey's brain,

body, and soul.

• On another note, our friends Erika and Manny of LivingSong (who graciously did a very successful benefit concert for us) are currently in Nashville with some ministry opportunities opening up to them. Please pray for God's wisdom and direction, and protection in their travels.

Thanks for all the prayers – every one of them!

Good night!

God is our refuge and strength, an ever-present help in trouble. Therefore we will not fear, though the earth give way and the mountains fall into the heart of the sea, though its waters roar and foam and the mountains quake with their surging. The Lord Almighty is with us; the God of Jacob is our fortress. He says, "Be still, and know that I am God; I will be exalted among the nations, I will be exalted in the earth." The Lord Almighty is with us; the God of Jacob is our fortress (Psalm 46:1-3, 7, 10, 11 NIV).

Miracle Man – Day 40

In PT today, Casey was jogging! jumping! and walking himself to the coffee shop downstairs to order a vanilla latte! :-) He had a fun time in PT today. In OT, they finally figured out how he likes his shower water – HOT! – so he enjoyed his shower very much today. :) And in Speech Therapy, he was writing short words prompted by the picture of each word, and he was spelling most words correctly! :-) We also celebrated Gary's (Casey's dad) birthday together over dinner, so it was a full day.

Our family met with the therapists and neuropsychologist today, as we are making preparations for Casey's return home. God has done so many amazing miracles in Casey's body in the past forty days, and we are continuing to believe that God will completely heal him…to God be the glory!

We need more miracles to happen, so please continue to pray:

• for COMPLETE healing of Casey's brain, body, and soul.
• for his vision to be fixed…it's very troublesome for him right now.
• that he understand when people talk to

237

him, and he speak the words he wants to say…that he conquer the aphasia!
• for wisdom for the family and all those caring for Casey and our boys.
• specifically for our four boys…"God, help them understand and trust You, even though Daddy has a lot of healing still to come."

I can't thank you enough for all the prayers and all your love! Good night!

There is no fear in love. But perfect love drives out fear, because fear has to do with punishment. The one who fears is not made perfect in love (1 John 4:18 NIV).

TUESDAY, MAY 20, 2014

Miracle Man – Day 41

Casey had a really great day today! I was so encouraged during my drive home this evening. :-) His blood pressure was low enough this morning that he didn't have to have his BP meds. That's a PTL! After lunch, he was telling me how much better he felt today. He was stronger, his right side felt better, his vision was better while still patching the right eye, his speech was better. He was all around...better! He was telling me that last night as he lay in bed, he felt like God was making him better. :-) PTL!!!

In PT, he was bowling, which was quite entertaining. I posted two videos on my Facebook page (Cindy Cleveland), one with him bowling with his right arm and another with his left. I also posted a short video clip of him in his hour-and-a-half speech session today. She's trying to work with him as much as she can before Casey goes home.

Tomorrow is Casey's last day of therapies at Joy Fuller Rehab Center. The staff and team have been amazing with him! We're so glad the Lord provided such a great facility so close to our home.

And speaking of home, Casey will be coming home on Thursday! That's great news, and it's a great opportunity to pray! Each transition over the past forty-one days has brought with it its own challenges. Although wonderful, going home is a BIG transition.

Specific prayers:
• Please pray for wisdom for me, the boys, and all the family as we care for Casey.
• Please pray for continued protection over Casey and all of us. As Casey prays every night, "No weapon formed against our family will prosper."

• Please pray for Casey to get the rest he needs as his brain continues to heal.

• Please pray for understanding for all of our amazingly wonderful friends and family that will want to visit him. Lord, help them understand that visits may be postponed or very brief, so as not to overstimulate Casey.

• Please pray for Casey's COMPLETE healing of his brain, body, and soul.

As always, thanks for the prayers. They're obviously working for Miracle Man, so please keep them going up!!!

Good night and God bless!

WHAT, THEN, SHALL WE SAY IN RESPONSE TO THESE THINGS?

IF GOD IS FOR US, WHO CAN BE AGAINST US? HE WHO DID NOT

SPARE HIS OWN SON, BUT GAVE HIM UP FOR US ALL

—HOW WILL HE NOT ALSO, ALONG WITH HIM, GRACIOUSLY

GIVE US ALL THINGS? (ROMANS 8:31, 32 NIV).

Miracle Man is Home! – Day 42

As I sit here on my bed writing this post (as I have for the past several weeks), there is something of great significance that is different about tonight. In the bed beside me is a wonderful, powerful man of God who is experiencing the miraculous power of Almighty God in his body! That's right—Casey is home!!! For the first time in 42 days! We are giving God much thanks!

Casey was scheduled to be discharged tomorrow morning, but due to scheduling changes, he was free to go home this evening, and we were all thrilled. :-)

Outpatient therapies will begin next week, and we continue to pray and believe for Casey's complete healing.

Prayers:
- Protection.
- Wisdom.
- Proper management of stimuli.
- Understanding for boys, family, and friends.
- COMPLETE healing for Casey's brain, body, and soul.

Now that Casey is home, I'm not sure I will be able to keep up with writing an update on this page every night. There will be other responsibilities, and maybe I'll figure out how to go to bed at a decent hour...So, for those you of that have told me you stay up so you can read the update on Casey each night, thanks so much, but just know there may not be a post every night.

Just for fun, I started keeping track over the past week how many visitors have come to Casey's page on a daily basis. On average, there are 127 visitors per day, that read about Miracle Man. So, for ALL of you that have supported us in so many ways, including opening up this website, reading about Casey's progress, praying, and/or sharing with others, WE say "THANK YOU!" Even on the hardest nights, it brought me so much encouragement when I would write about Casey's day, knowing that there were so many of you supporting and loving on us. So again—"THANK YOU!"

Until next time, keep praying and believing...

Good night!

<u>Miracle Man - Day 46</u>

I haven't had much free time lately but thought I would write a quick update on Miracle Man now that he's home. :-) He has been adjusting well to being at home, which has included long rest times during the day. In effort to keep Casey from being overly stimulated, we have changed the boys' routine a bit, and everyone has been very accommodating (most of the time!).

Today, Casey started asking some questions that brought about a quality conversation. He wondered how many pounds he's lost (30-40 pounds). He asked how long ago all of this started (about 6.5 weeks ago). Of course to him, it feels like it's been forever…When I showed him a picture of his incision, I think it all started to make sense to him. He realized why so much of his body has changed. And he was okay with the need to lie around and rest his brain.

He also asked if we know what caused the stroke. On a spiritual level, we see it as a direct attack of our enemy, the devil. Physically, we don't know what caused the stroke. Three suggestions come to mind: 1. high blood pressure (which he did not have at a doctor's visit a year ago…) 2. over-activity (he was involved in a big project at the time) 3. it may have been something he was born with. We don't know the

243

answer to his question, but we do know we're going to get through this, with God helping us every step of the way!

Mega-thanks to his former PT Craig for giving us the idea to place a decal on his glasses as a patch. Casey is pleased with his ability to see out of his left eye when his right eye is patched.

Prayers needed:
• VISION—continues to be a challenge, and I am working to connect him with the right neuro-ophthalmologist. Please pray for wisdom, open doors, and financial provision.
• COMMUNICATION—although he seems to be improving, it's still a challenge at times to find the right word, as well as understand what's being said to him.
• COMPLETE HEALING of Casey's brain, body, and soul.

Thanks again for all the prayers, love, and support!

Many evils confront the [consistently] righteous, but the Lord delivers him out of them all (Psalm 34:19 AMP).

Miracle Man – Day 47

It appears Miracle Man received a miraculous touch of God today! I don't know the experience of other stroke victims when (or if) they get the feeling back on their affected side, but for Casey, it appeared to be nothing short of a miracle! We ate Memorial Day lunch at his parents' house. (This was the first time Casey had been back to their house since the stroke.) After enjoying some delicious shrimp tacos and bread pudding, Casey was walking around the family room. As soon as he sat down to rest, he could feel the muscle spasm in his right leg. Even after the muscles calmed down, he still could feel his whole right side! For now, it's very sensitive, and at times painful to the touch, but he realizes it's a good pain. It's God healing him, and we're so grateful!

Thanks for the continued prayers—they're working, so keep them going up! And as you pray for Casey, please thank God for all He's already done for Casey and for all He's still going to do!

Good night!

The secret [of the sweet, satisfying companionship] of the Lord have they who fear (revere and worship) Him, and He will show them His covenant and reveal to them its [deep, inner] meaning (Psalm 25:14 AMP).

245

<u>Miracle Man – Day 53</u>

Just a quick update to say Casey has made significant progress again this past week, for which we give God much thanks! He has started to feel his right side again, which enabled him to play his guitar this week. The songs are coming back to him and it's beautiful! :) On Thursday night, his sister Rhea brought him over to the praise band rehearsal, and Casey had the delight of seeing and hearing for the first time the completion of the new stage and sound system in the sanctuary at Shepherd's Community United Methodist Church. You see, just prior to his stroke on April 9, Casey and his team were working tirelessly on the new stage and sound system. The design was his creation, and Thursday he was able to see his vision completed! It was an awesome, glorious moment for all involved!

Today he spent most of the day with his eye patch off because his vision is improving! That's a great big PRAISE THE LORD! From what I understand, the double vision issue is starting to be not so much an issue. His eyes are coming into alignment, and it's a beautiful thing!!!

Continued prayers, please:
• for his vision to continue to line up so he doesn't see double, and for any blindness

(right hemianopsia) to be cleared up.

• for his speech and comprehension to continue to improve.

• for Casey as he starts outpatient therapy tomorrow in Winter Haven.

• for Casey's COMPLETE healing of his brain, body, and soul.

Thanks so much, and may God richly bless you all!

I WILL bless the Lord at all times; His praise shall continually be in my mouth. My life makes its boast in the Lord; let the humble and afflicted hear and be glad. O magnify the Lord with me, and let us exalt His name together. I sought (inquired of) the Lord and required Him [of necessity and on the authority of His Word], and He heard me, and delivered me from all my fears (Psalm 34:1-4 AMP).

<u>Miracle Man – Day 60</u>

The highlight of the week for me was seeing Casey at the church service this morning at Shepherd's Community UMC! This was a milestone for Casey, and we were so thrilled to have him there. He even stayed for the whole service (and it was a long one! :-)) He raised his arms and worshiped our God as he sang a beautiful melody, although the words do not come to him quickly enough yet. But they will, and he'll be singing his praises from the stage again…

He survived three days of outpatient therapies this past week, and has two days scheduled for this week, as well as an MRI tomorrow, followed by a visit to see his neurosurgeon on Tuesday. It will be a full week!

Continued prayers appreciated for…
• MRI tomorrow—peace, no stress or complications, and a good report!
• wisdom for the neurosurgeon as he follows up with Casey. May God's name be praised as Dr. Lau sees the progress (a.k.a. miracles) Casey is experiencing.
• strength and continued progress in therapies.
• his vision to be healed completely. He talks of his vision changing, so something is hap-

pening—which is good.
• his speech and understanding to improve and be completely restored.
• Casey's COMPLETE healing of his brain, body, and soul.

Continued thanks for all the prayers, love, encouraging words, cards, gifts, meals, financial blessings, babysitting, etc. Thanks for being interested enough in what God is doing in our family to read this! :-)

God bless you all!

The salvation of the righteous comes from the Lord; he is their stronghold in time of trouble. The Lord helps them and delivers them; he delivers them from the wicked and saves them, because they take refuge in him (Psalm 37:39, 40 NIV).

Miracle Man – Day 67

Happy Father's Day to all you dads out there! We give much thanks to our Heavenly Father for allowing Casey to be alive and well on this Father's Day!

Thanks to all of who prayed for Casey last week as he had an MRI on Monday. Your prayers for peace were answered! He did great! It was a "high field open MRI" with forty-five minutes of loud rattling sounds. He lay there and smiled the whole time. :-)

On Tuesday, we had a follow-up with the neurosurgeon, Dr. Lau. His first comment to Casey was, "Wow Casey! You look much better than you did in the hospital!" :-) Dr. Lau's comments were encouraging, and he only expects Casey to continue to improve.

Casey's therapies this week went well...continued progress...continued thanks!

Casey has been sharing from his heart this week, and I wish you all could hear him. He really is truly in love with his Savior Jesus Christ, and he wants to tell anyone who will listen of the love Jesus has for each of us. He repeatedly says, "God is so good."

Prayers:
• Casey's COMPLETE healing of his brain, body, and soul.

• Vision is still changing every day, which is good. Pray for the double vision to come together and be one, and there be no fields of blindness.

• Communication is improving. Pray he understand what's being said to him, and he be able to say the words he wants to say.

• Meeting with neurologist on Wednesday. Please pray for wisdom for him, especially in regards to what medications he's taking.

• Pray for wisdom for family as we consider hyperbaric oxygen therapy for him.

• Pray for strength for us all.

Thanks and may God richly bless you all!

AND MAY THE GOD OF PEACE HIMSELF SANCTIFY YOU THROUGH AND THROUGH [SEPARATE YOU FROM PROFANE THINGS, MAKE YOU PURE AND WHOLLY CONSECRATED TO GOD]; AND MAY YOUR SPIRIT AND SOUL AND BODY BE PRESERVED SOUND AND COMPLETE [AND FOUND] BLAMELESS AT THE COMING OF OUR LORD JESUS CHRIST (THE MESSIAH). FAITHFUL IS HE WHO IS CALLING YOU [TO HIMSELF] AND UTTERLY TRUSTWORTHY, AND HE WILL ALSO DO IT [FULFILL HIS CALL BY HALLOWING AND KEEPING YOU]

(1 THESSALONIANS 5:23, 24 AMP).

<u>Miracle Man – Day 71</u>

You know Casey is feeling better because today was the first time since his stroke that he changed a poopy diaper!!! He is actually starting to become quite helpful around the house, which is great because I need all the help I can get! :-)

On Monday, he said he wanted to pray that his eyes would improve enough that he could remove the eye patch within the week. Today he woke up early, and his vision was even better than yesterday, and he was able to spend a good portion of the day without the patch. PTL! He has his first appointment with a neuro-ophthalmologist on Monday, so please pray for wisdom of us and him.

His appointment with the neurologist yesterday went very well. The doctor recognizes that God has given Casey another chance to live, and oh, how we are all very grateful!

On a personal family note, I am counting our many blessings. Today was the first time in quite a while that I went grocery shopping. Between yummy meals being provided and other kindhearted people making grocery runs for us, we have been well taken care of. And then, to top it off, our whole grocery bill was covered by the generous Publix gift cards given by more wonderful, loving people…and I still have more gift cards for future trips! :-) I can't say enough "thank you"s and "God bless you"s to the amazing support system that has helped us every step of the way through this journey. Thank you. Thank you. Thank you.

And may my God richly bless you all!!!

O give thanks unto the Lord, call upon His name, make known His doings among the peoples! Sing to Him, sing praises to Him; meditate on and talk of all His marvelous deeds and devoutly praise them (Psalm 105:1, 2 AMP).

Miracle Man – Day 100

Let me start by saying "Thanks!" to all of you who have walked along beside us over the past one hundred days. Some of you have literally been at our side; others have followed at a distance and have kept up by reading the Caring Bridge entries. We know many of you have prayed for us often (and even daily) because we have felt the prayers and seen many, many miracles! Some of you have joined us partway through this journey, so allow me to do a quick recap of the past one hundred days...

At 4:30 a.m. on April 9, 2014, I was awakened to Casey speaking (in the spiritual realm) saying "No, God!" and speaking out to Jesus. What followed were flu-like symptoms and some delusional talking. Approximately twelve hours later, he was having emergency brain surgery to remove a large blood clot that had formed on the left side of his brain as a result of a hemorrhagic stroke. Surgery was very successful, and Casey spent the next fifteen days receiving extraordinary care in the Trauma Intensive Care Unit at Lakeland Regional Medical Center, followed by four more days in a "regular" room at LRMC before being transported to Joy Fuller Rehab Center in Winter Haven Hospital, where he spent the next three and a half weeks. At the rehab center, he received three hours of therapy a day, including Physical Therapy—where he was taught how to walk again and keep his balance; Occupational Therapy—where he was taught how to shower and brush his teeth and worked on strengthening his right side which was weakened by the stroke; and Speech Therapy—where he was taught how to communicate while dealing with aphasia.

On his six-week mark (Day 42), Casey returned home, and what a glorious day that was!!! He started outpatient rehab in the Esteem program at Winter Haven Hospital. On Day 85, he had reached all of his goals for PT and was discharged from the program. He continues to work on OT and Speech Therapy. On Day 97, Casey started Hyperbaric Oxygen Therapy every weekday in Winter Park for approximately twenty sessions.

Physically, Casey is strong and he can take care of his personal needs. His greatest challenges are his speech (understanding and speaking correctly) and his vision, which seems to be changing every day. The neuro-ophthalmologist said Casey's vision could continue to change for about a year, and told us to come back to see him in April 2015.

It is obvious to me that God's hand remains upon Casey's life! Before surgery on April 9, the neurosurgeon was NOT overly optimistic that Casey would survive, much less have a quality lifestyle. We have witnessed many, many miracles, in addition to the fact that Casey is young and DETERMINED! And, in case you're wondering, Casey's sense of humor has remained intact, and he is often causing us to laugh!

THEN THEY CRIED TO THE LORD IN THEIR TROUBLE, AND HE SAVED THEM FROM THEIR DISTRESS. HE SENT OUT HIS WORD AND HEALED THEM; HE RESCUED THEM FROM THE GRAVE. LET THEM GIVE THANKS TO THE LORD FOR HIS UNFAILING LOVE AND HIS WONDERFUL DEEDS FOR MANKIND. LET THEM SACRIFICE THANK OFFERINGS AND TELL OF HIS WORKS WITH SONGS OF JOY (PSALM 107:19-22 NIV).

Miracle Man – HBO Therapy Report

Today Casey goes to Winter Park for his fifteenth hyperbaric oxygen therapy treatment. We will conclude with eighteen treatments on Thursday, and we are super-excited about having our family back together again, without the daily three hours on the road. A mini family getaway is planned for this weekend to celebrate!

Many have asked how the treatments have been going, so here are the obvious results:

1. Casey's right side has been "coming back to life," and sometimes it's very painful!

2. A couple times this weekend I was talking to him about some detailed events. He seemed to understand what I was saying, so I asked him, "Are you understanding everything I'm saying?", and he thought about it and said, "Yeah, I guess so!" With aphasia, the input/output is challenged, so understanding what is said to him and finding the right words to say is sometimes difficult. But we're experiencing more moments of him understanding which is fabulous! And I think his output speech is improving, too!

3. His vision is still constantly changing, which is still good. His close-up vision is better than his distant, which still suffers from double vision. Also, the blindness on his right side needs to go so he can see every-

257

thing (and eventually drive again!).

Many of you have also asked how you can help. As always, prayers are constantly appreciated! Not only for Casey, but please pray for me (Cindy)—I need it! We have four very active young boys that need a healed daddy and a not-so-weary mommy. Thanks for the prayers!

Hyperbaric Oxygen Therapy is a form of "alternative medicine." Casey is in a chamber breathing in 100% oxygen for sixty minutes each treatment. (We are breathing only 21% oxygen normally.) The purpose is for the oxygen to enter his body, particularly his plasma, and infiltrate life and healing to damaged cells. Recent research from Tel Aviv shows improvement for those who participated, and we are believing for COMPLETE healing for Casey's brain, body, and soul. We trust HBO Therapy is part of that healing process, so that's why we're driving to Winter Park (the other side of Orlando) five days a week. If you find this to be a worthy cause and are able to help cover the costs, please consider giving to our online donation page or mail us a check if you prefer.

Here's how it breaks down:

1 Full HBO Therapy treatment: $135

1/2 treatment: $67.50

1/4 treatment: $33.75

We have nine more treatments to pay for later this week, so if you desire and are able to help cover the costs, that would be marvelous! I know it never hurts to ask, so I'm asking… :-)

May my God bless you all for your love and support to our family. You all have been an encouragement and a ray of hope at some of our darkest moments. Thank you for being here for us.

May the God of your hope so fill you with all joy and peace in believing [through the experience of your faith] that by the power of the Holy Spirit you may abound and be overflowing (bubbling over) with hope (Romans 15:13 AMP).

Miracle Man – Day 130

We've reached a few milestones since my last update, so here we go…

1. Casey completed eighteen hyperbaric oxygen therapy treatments over the course of four weeks, which meant we spent many long days driving back and forth from Winter Park. Many, many thanks to all of you who prayed for our travels and who gave so generously toward the treatments. We had no out-of-pocket costs for treatments, and your generous gifts also helped toward our meals and gas along the way. Thanks a ton! You may be asking, "Did the HBO Therapy help?" Well, it seems to be…Casey's right side continues to "come alive," or as he describes it, it's "on fire"! Also, he can now feel his right foot when he moves it! His vision, speech, and understanding continue to improve. In fact, the last few days driving to and from HBOT, we had some great conversations in the car, which previously had been difficult to do without the use of eye contact and writing pads. We continue to give thanks to God for every miracle and every progression.

2. We had our first family getaway since Casey's stroke four months ago! In our travels down I-4 to HBOT, I had hoped and prayed that we could have a family "reunion" at Gaylord Palms after the completion of his treatments. And that's exactly what happened— God is so good to us! After Casey's final oxygen treat-

ment, our family and some friends spent two nights at Gaylord Palms, and then Casey's WONDERFUL mom and sister brought the four boys home so Casey and I could enjoy an evening alone. Other than the over-priced food, Gaylord Palms was a perfect choice for our family and a dream come true!

3. Casey reached the four-month mark, and he is so much farther along than anyone could have ever predicted. Thank You, Jesus! We were enjoying a dinner out, celebrating our lives together, when Casey wasn't quite understanding what I was saying to him. He cordially apologized for his lack of understanding. I responded by reminding him that four months ago at that moment, he had his skull opened up having major brain surgery! Although he often gets frustrated with his limitations, he knows God has brought him very far down a very long journey, so we continue to count our blessings...

4. Today was a major milestone as Casey played his guitar in our church service at Shepherd's Community UMC for the first time since his stroke! Prior to April 9, Casey was our worship leader. Since then, I have led our amazing team, and today, Casey joined us again as a leader on the stage! I am overjoyed!!! Although the words to the songs don't come quickly enough for him yet, he is able to play his guitar, which is really amazing and great therapy. We are going to start working on "O Holy Night" so he can have that

song ready for Christmas Eve! :-) To God be the glory…

5. Finally, our family has accepted what appears to be a major blessing from the Lord. First Methodist School in Bartow offered me a part-time teaching position which will allow me to teach music two days a week, and give Casey and me three days a week to develop his skills. Solomon (3rd grade), Isaac (2nd), and Daniel (3-year-olds) all start school tomorrow. I will start teaching in September, and Josiah will start school in October when he turns two! Until now, I have homeschooled Solomon and Isaac, but the thought of homeschooling right now with our situation seems a bit overwhelming. So I'm so grateful to God and the school for providing this amazing opportunity for us at this time!

Thanks to all of you who stuck with me through this very long update! :-) I hope you find as much delight as I do seeing and reading about what God is doing in our Miracle Man! To God be the glory, great things He has done…

> Praise the Lord. Give thanks to the Lord, for he is good; his love endures forever. Who can proclaim the mighty acts of the Lord or fully declare his praise? (Psalm 106:1, 2 NIV).

<u>Thanksgiving Weekend Edition</u>

It's been quite a while since I've posted an update on Caring Bridge concerning Casey's progress. He's doing great, and as we close out Thanksgiving weekend 2014, I just wanted to share a few "thanksgivings."

• We are most grateful to God our Father and the Lord Jesus Christ for the Holy Spirit's healing power that has been and continues to flow throughout Casey's body, completing one miracle after another. Some more miracles to be seen would be vision completely restored (specifically his right peripheral), feeling being restored to his right side, and understanding speech and speaking correctly.

• We are so very grateful that Casey is alive and well! Casey is a fighter, and he is determined that God still has good plans for him to accomplish here on this earth.

• Our hearts are filled with gratitude for each one of you! Thank you for standing with us, believing for us, praying for us, and supporting us every step of this journey.

I had a lot more I wanted to write about, but I'm too tired...must get some sleep... :)

Good night.

Praise the Lord. Give thanks to the Lord, for he is good; his love endures forever (Psalm 106:1 NIV).

FRIDAY, DECEMBER 5, 2014

Casey's 41st Birthday Edition
You appreciate life more
When you've been at death's door.

As a forty-year-old, Casey Cleveland was at death's door after experiencing a massive bleed on his brain (hemorrhagic stroke). The hours and days following his stroke were filled with many questions, including ones like "Will Casey live to see his next birthday?" and "if so, what condition will he be in...paralyzed, brain dead, healed?" I am THRILLED to report that Casey is alive and well and on the road to COMPLETE healing!!!

Casey has fought hard over the past almost-eight months, and we give God great praise for His continued healing touch and for His allowing us to celebrate another year with Casey! I often wonder at what point will the effects of the stroke not stare us in the face every single day. Do you know what I mean? For instance, the day Casey starts driving again will be a huge day of victory, because that will mean his vision (specifically his right peripheral) will be restored. When Casey's right side has regained all feeling and it's no longer "on fire"…that'll be a reason to celebrate! And his speech…that's the most challenging…The days are coming when I will speak to him, and he will understand what I'm saying, every time. And he will find the right words to say every time. Although these victories are yet to be seen and the results of the stroke stare us in the face every day, we celebrate the major victories that Casey has experienced…the fact he walks and talks at all is a major blessing!

So today is Casey's 41st birthday, and that gives us all great reason to celebrate! If you're on Facebook, please consider writing him a post on his page today. If you have his phone number, give him a call or send a text. Or send him an email at caseyjcleveland@gmail.com. I know he would be delighted to hear from you all on his special day.

Casey has been unable to work a "job" since his stroke, but he plans to take up video production again in the not-too-far future. That requires a professional-grade camera, which is several thousands of dollars.

He's been searching the internet for the best deals. So, we're asking all who wish to participate to consider giving a financial gift toward his camera, so Casey can start working again. Since he's 41 today, maybe you would want to give a gift in any increment using 41...$4.10, $41, $410...or put as many "zeros" as you'd like (heehee!). There's no pressure to give, just a suggestion if you'd like to contribute toward the next phase of Casey's development...vocational. Once again, no pressure, just a suggestion...

Please pray for Casey today. Thanks and have a great day and a joyous holiday season!

Happily married to Miracle Man,

Cindy

[What, what would have become of me] had I not believed that I would see the Lord's goodness in the land of the living! Wait and hope for and expect the Lord; be brave and of good courage and let your heart be stout and enduring. Yes, wait for and hope for and expect the Lord (Psalm 27:13, 14 AMP).

Nine Month edition

It's been nine months since Casey's stroke, and he continues to improve and live up to his name—"Miracle Man." He accomplished an amazing goal this Christmas season as he sang "O Holy Night" in three public performances. (A quick backstory: Casey has sung "O Holy Night" for years, and his singing has been a holiday highlight for many. A week or so after his stroke, when we were unsure if he could still sing, his parents, our pastor, and I declared that Casey would sing "O Holy Night" again this year.)

With speech aphasia, even reading the lyrics of the song was a huge challenge for Casey. He started working on the words in speech therapy about six weeks before his first performance. It took nearly the whole forty-five-minute session for him just to read aloud through the two verses and two choruses. That gives you an idea of what he had to overcome. Then there's singing the right notes in time with the music...breathing... standing properly...etc. Praise be to God—he did it! And he did it beautifully!

Here's the link to his performance on Christmas Eve at Shepherd's Community Church. It's not a flawless performance, but nonetheless AMAZING! Enjoy!

http://m.youtube.com/watch?v=5Pc__o8rr5s

The Lord has been so gracious to us in many ways, one of which is the opportunity to share our story with others using mass media. Over the past month, we have had the privilege of sharing our story on two radio programs as well as in the local newspaper. Here are the links…

One J.A.M. Nation 12/28/2014

http://www.wtis1110.com/ShowPages-ShowTemp/one-jam-nation/2014-12-28_OneJamNation_Archive.mp3

The Pete O'Shea Show 1/2/2015 (We are halfway through this program at the 1-hour mark.)

http://www.wtis1110.com/ShowPages-ShowTemp/the-pete-oshea-show/2015-01-02_ThePeteOSheaShow_Archive.m…

The Ledger 1/18/2015

http://www.theledger.com/article/20150118/NEWS/150119397?p=1&tc=pg

Thanks for reading, listening, and praying! Please continue to believe with me that Casey will be completed healed of speech aphasia (communication challenges), vision deficits, and feeling on right side…COMPLETELY healed—brain, body, and soul!

I remain confident of this: I will see the goodness of the Lord in the land of the living. Wait for the Lord; be strong and take heart and wait for the Lord (Psalm 27:13, 14 NIV).

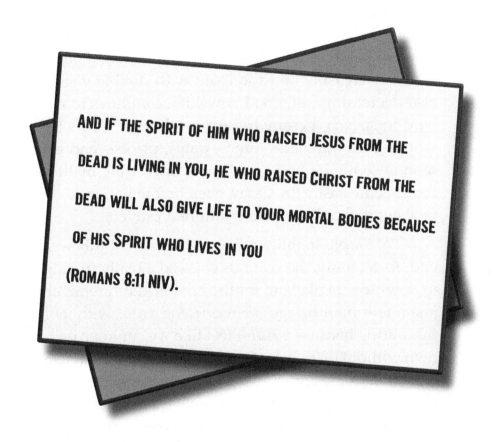

AND IF THE SPIRIT OF HIM WHO RAISED JESUS FROM THE DEAD IS LIVING IN YOU, HE WHO RAISED CHRIST FROM THE DEAD WILL ALSO GIVE LIFE TO YOUR MORTAL BODIES BECAUSE OF HIS SPIRIT WHO LIVES IN YOU (ROMANS 8:11 NIV).

<u>Eleven Month update</u>

I haven't written an update in a while. You know the saying, "No news is good news." And that's true with our story, too. Our good news is that Casey continues to improve! The feeling on his right side is starting to come back more and more. :-) His vision continues to change, which means the blind spot in his right peripheral is decreasing and the issue with double vision is also decreasing...all good news! He continues to work hard in speech therapy twice a week. Lately, he's been working on numbers—times, dates, prices—and even more recently on basic math problems. Well, math has never come easily for Casey, even before his stroke. But he'll get it, thanks to your continued prayers!

A couple highlights for me happened this weekend. As a family, the six of us enjoyed a really fun night in downtown Lakeland for the First Friday. I remember just a few months ago a close friend went with us for this outing because I didn't feel like we could go on our own without extra help. But this weekend we did it and had a marvelous time! Also, for the first time this weekend, Casey watched our four boys by himself for over three hours! Which allowed me to go enjoy some much-needed girl time! :-)

We continue to give God great thanks for His gracious healing upon Casey and His great faithfulness to our family. Thanks for your continued prayers:

- for COMPLETE healing for Casey, brain, body, and soul.
- for his right side to continue to get its feeling back.
- for his vision for be completely restored. We're scheduled to see his neuro- ophthalmologist the end of April. We pray at some point he will be clear to drive again.
- for his communication skills—that he would understand what's being said to him, he would have the right words to say, and his understanding of numbers would improve.
- that God would use Casey's story to give hope and encouragement to all who need to hear it!

Thanks for journeying with us!

I LOVE You fervently and devotedly, O Lord, my Strength. The Lord is my Rock, my Fortress, and my Deliverer; my God, my keen and firm Strength in Whom I will trust and take refuge, my Shield, and the Horn of my salvation, my High Tower. I will call upon the Lord, Who is to be praised; so shall I be saved from my enemies. The cords or bands of death surrounded me, and the streams of ungodliness and the torrents of ruin terrified me. The cords of Sheol (the place of the dead) surrounded me; the snares of death confronted and came upon me. In my distress [when seemingly closed in] I called upon the Lord and cried to my God; He heard my voice out of His temple (heavenly dwelling place), and my cry came before Him, into His [very] ears. As for God, His way is perfect! The word of the Lord is tested and tried; He is a shield to all those who take refuge and put their trust in Him (Psalm 18:1-6, 30 AMP).

THURSDAY, APRIL 9, 2015

Miracle Man – Day 365

April 9, 2014, was the day Casey had a massive hemorrhagic stroke. He started showing signs of it at 4:30 a.m., so as I contemplate the events of last year at this very moment, my heart is filled with gratitude. I am most grateful, first of all to our God, for He has sustained, healed, and provided in countless ways. I am grateful for each of you who has stood with us along this journey; we have felt your support in countless ways...cards, gifts, financial support, encouraging words, meals, babysitters, hugs, prayers, etc. From the bottom of our hearts, THANK YOU! I am so grateful for the medical staff that has cared for Casey over the past year—every doctor, nurse, technician, therapist, etc. I give God special thanks today for Dr. Lau, who performed emergency surgery on Casey's brain, excavating the blood that had leaked into his brain. Dr. Lau did an AMAZING job…thank You, Lord!

Thank you for your continued prayers for Casey's COMPLETE healing—brain, body, and soul…

> *And remember, "And if the Spirit of him who raised Jesus from the dead is living in you, he who raised Christ from the dead will also give life to your mortal bodies because of his Spirit who lives in you" (Romans 8:11 NIV).*

Have a blessed day!

Cindy (happily married to Miracle Man!)

Two Year Update

I have attempted on several occasions over the past year to write an update, but none of those have materialized, and now it's been another year since Casey had a hemorrhagic stroke. So what's happened over the past year, you might ask...

Casey continues to improve! PTL! Improvements are at a much slower rate, which frustrates Casey at times, but for the most part, he has had such a great attitude throughout this whole life-changing situation. He still gets "stuck" on some words that would be very natural for most of us to say, but when that happens, we often find ourselves laughing at the words he comes up with, which makes the struggle more manageable. For example, today we were talking about music, and he was trying to say the word "lyrics" but the word "lizard" came out instead! That gave us a good laugh!

He still deals with burning sensations on his right side. When it's really intense, he describes it as feeling "on fire," and this past week, that feeling lasted for several days which can be exhausting.

Other than the blind spot that currently remains in his right peripheral, his vision is basically back to normal. He has an eye appointment scheduled for Monday, so please pray all goes well and that the doctor will clear him to drive again.

274

Roughly six months ago, when Casey saw his PCP, Dr. Cardona said, "I think you're going to make a full recovery!" That's what we've been praying and believing for, right?!?! It was so encouraging to hear his doctor say that!

We are in the process of planning a Celebration for all God has done in healing Casey, as well as a couple other Miracles that have walked a similar journey. We are making plans now and will let you know when and where that Celebration will be. Sure hope you will celebrate with us!

> And remember, "And if the Spirit of him who raised Jesus from the dead is living in you, he who raised Christ from the dead will also give life to your mortal bodies because of his Spirit who lives in you" (Romans 8:11 NIV).

Be blessed and keep your eyes on Jesus, Who's been so good to us!

Blessings,

Cindy (happily married to Miracle Man)

P.S. On this two-year anniversary, would you consider writing a word of encouragement to Casey in the comments below or on his Facebook page? An extra special treat for him would be a video posted to his FB page or texted to him, if you have his cell number. Thanks in advance for helping to make today a special day for him.

MAY THE GOD OF YOUR HOPE SO FILL YOU WITH ALL JOY AND PEACE

IN BELIEVING [THROUGH THE EXPERIENCE OF YOUR FAITH] THAT BY

THE POWER OF THE HOLY SPIRIT YOU MAY ABOUND AND BE

OVERFLOWING (BUBBLING OVER) WITH HOPE

(ROMANS 15:13 AMPC).

<u>Five Year Update</u>

April 9, 2019 – Today marks five years since Casey had a hemorrhagic stroke. As I consider the events of five years ago, I am humbled and grateful for how God has sustained us and led us to where we are today.

Five years ago, I woke up to Casey showing signs of having the flu or food poisoning, only to find out later in the day that he suffered a major hemorrhagic stroke in the early hours of the morning. By 4:30 p.m., he was being prepped for brain surgery to extract the blood that had accumulated in his brain.

Many of you walked the long journey with us…

…the uncertainty of those first few days;

…the 15 days in the TICU;

…the difficult transition to a regular room at LRMC;

…the 3-1/2 weeks at the inpatient rehab center;

…his re-learning how to walk, talk, brush his teeth, play his guitar, etc.;

…his exciting, yet challenging, transition back home;

…weeks of travel to hyperbaric oxygen therapy;

…our journey into a "new normal" as a family.

Day after day, you—Casey's Army—would pray prayers of faith for Casey's COMPLETE healing. My consistent response was "Thank you, and keep the prayers going up…they're working!"

Five years later, I can attest to the power of prayer and God's faithfulness in our lives. Prayer works and Jesus is real!!!

Casey's perseverance has been amazing to watch…

…Although he still does not feel the whole right side of his body, he continues to move and trust with each step he takes.

…Although his peripheral vision still keeps him from driving, he has such grace and patience being transported by myself and others.

…And it's a real treat to listen to him communicate—even if he can't think of the right word to say, he can get very creative at describing what he's trying to say, which often leads us to laughter.

Laughter is good medicine. It has indeed helped Casey recover and not take himself too seriously.

So, what's he up to these days, you might ask.

I'm so proud of him. Casey is an amazing man of God who loves Jesus, loves me, and loves his precious boys very much! He's taken up the role of cooking dinner most nights, which is certainly helpful for me, as I drive children to and from school, practices, lessons, etc.

Just recently, Casey finished recording his first song since his stroke. You can find it on iTunes, Spotify, Amazon, etc. Just search for Casey J Cleveland, "Still Worthy." It's a beautiful song written after our daughter Selah was stillborn. Casey J Cleveland is working on another recording, so keep him in mind when you're searching for music.

Here's the Amazon link:

https://www.amazon.com/Still-Worthy-Casey-J-Cleveland/dp/B07NJ3GW2M/ref=sr_1_2?keywords=Casey+J+Cleveland&qid=1550093109&s=gateway&sr=8-2

Casey and I have continued to serve together as worship leaders. Although we are not currently serving on a weekly basis at a church service, we have the awesome and unique privilege of leading worship at special events and women's retreats and conferences. Here's what's so super cool about these events—all four of our boys participate with us on the worship team! It's super awesome worshiping our great God and leading worship altogether as a family!

In addition to leading worship together, Casey and I have the privilege of sharing our story of hope at various events, including retreats, conferences, luncheons, church services, etc.

I've been writing our story, so it will be in book form in the months ahead!

And for my "day job," I teach music (particularly piano) at various schools and at home, too.

A lot has changed for us in five years, but what we have witnessed with God's faithfulness and His provision have been nothing less than miraculous.

Thanks to all who have stood with us, supported us, loved us, and prayed for us.

And a great big shout-out to Casey's awesome family! His sister Rhea has been very supportive and understanding, especially during his early adjustments. His mom and dad (Tee and Gary) have loved on us in ways beyond what I could have ever expected ...but obviously needed! Thank you, Mom and Dad C.

Oftentimes, I would conclude our journal entries on Caring Bridge with a list of prayers and a Bible verse, so here goes...

PRAYER:
• that God would use our family mightily to grow His Kingdom

Blessings,

Cindy (*still* happily married to Miracle Man)

Each year on Cathy's birthday we find different ways to celebrate her life. On September 16, 2018—her forty-seventh birthday—I encouraged any friends on Facebook to write a favorite memory of Cathy. Here are a few of the posts that were shared by such sweet family and friends.

Cheryl I. – Happy heavenly birthday, sweet Cathy! She was the epitome of a loving graceful woman of God. So soft spoken and always an encourager to all! When I hear an ambulance or any emergency vehicle, I remember when Cathy and Tripp and Lauren Ashley were in the dental office and she got with the kids and stopped and prayed for whoever was in need. She is fine of course but sure is missed. Love to all the family.

Kristin L. – When I was probably in 9th grade at Evangel, I really noticed her on stage one day. I noticed how beautiful she was…not because of physical beauty but to see God shine through her…and shine through her beautiful smile. And I had one of those life changing moments where you make a decision. And I decided I would smile. Not just when I was happy and things were great, but all the time.

And that I would aim to let God shine through me, even when I don't feel very shiny. I got a chance to tell her on FB message when we first became virtual friends :) It is amazing to me how God can shine through us even when we don't know anyone is watching. He certainly radiated through Cathy Pike Asbridge

Donna B. – There was never a day that Cathy didn't give her beautiful smile! As her teacher, I learned from her how to be positive and giving in all circumstances. The fond memories of Cathy still bless me!

Joanna P. – If I am ever struggling in worship or prayer, I see Cathy with her smile worshipping God with all her heart. It makes me stronger having known her.

Julie R. – Cathy was a beautiful example of a godly woman with a gentle and quiet spirit. Her joy and love for Jesus was radiant.

Clark G. – I'll never forget her beautiful smile no matter where I saw her.

Susan S. – Cathy is in a group picture from a mission trip to Merida that I keep on my bookshelf. My thoughts are never far from her. She was sweetness and life and the most Godly woman I'd ever met. Her loving tenderness, not only to her children, but to all she met, touched my soul in a profound way that I can never forget. Thanks, Cindy, for prompting us to remember. Your spirit is hers. ☐☐

Sonya C. – I have many fond memories of such a wonderful person and friend! Cathy was a great example of Jesus!

Ann Marie P. – STILL CELEBRATING YOUR IMPACT ON LIVES!

Wanda S. – Happy heavenly birthday sweet Cathy! I love you and I miss you so much!

Yvonne F. – What a beautiful woman inside and out. That picture captures her essence that we still feel with us. So grateful for her friendship, her love, her grace and generosity. I've never known anyone like her. Can't even express how moved I am even today to see her radiant joy! She loved JESUS and only ever wanted to draw others to Him.

Michelle R. – I remember when Cathy and Yvonne F. and I went to the Billy Graham Crusade in Tampa together. All 3 of us had just had babies. Cathy brought Tripp along and he was very colicky. Cried the whole way there and back. Our babies did not have colic so we had not experienced this level of constant crying. Cathy smiled (exhaustedly) the entire time. I haven't seen anything like it before or since. That smile was constant and sincere. Just thinking of it makes me smile too.

Beth R. – Our precious Cathy was both my student and my friend. Although I was nine years older, I always wanted to be like her when I grew up! What a testimony her life was to everyone who knew her or even knew of her. She was truly the hands and feet of Jesus. I still miss her yearly phone calls at 12:01 am on February 19th to be the first to wish me a Happy Birthday. You are loved, Cathy, and you will never be forgotten!

For Cathy's 48th birthday, a gentleman who helped Cathy through her pageant years wrote these very kind words about her:

Rob L. — Yesterday was this Angel's Birthday. I miss her every day! Before she was an amazing Wife, Mother, Teacher, and Mentor, she was an incredible Pageant Contestant! Intelligent, beautiful, and one of the most talented Flutist I've ever seen in Pageants! This girl did not stand still and play, she danced and moved around the stage, smiled and used her eyes to entertain while not missing a beat on the flute! She competed at the State Pageant 3 Times and made the top 10 every year! She had such a servant's heart and was so kind and loving! Because of our relationship, she became a mentor to Miss Florida 2008. It's been 8 years since she left us but she remains in my heart! I truly hope her 4 beautiful children know what a wonder women their Mother was during her short stay on this earth. Miss you, Cathy Pike!

In early 2019, I came in contact with a friend of Cathy's from her high school years. James Ridgway agreed to allow me share the letter he had written to my parents after Cathy's passing.

February 23, 2019

Mr. and Mrs. Pike,

Recently, I reconnected with Cindy through an email interchange which included my brother-in-law. It was nice to catch up on the Pike family, and I was delighted to know that both of you are doing well...after all of these years.

I mentioned to Cindy that I had composed a letter to you just after Cathy's passing eight years ago but for one reason or another I never sent it, and as time passed I did not even know if you still lived at the house I remembered from high school. So I was delighted to know that I could send you these reflections after all of these years. Frankly, nothing has changed in my mind since I wrote this years ago.

Sincerely,

James Ridgway

April 2011
Dear Mr. and Mrs. Pike,

My sincere condolences to you and your family on the passing of Cathy this past week. I was so disappointed to be out of town on Friday as I had hoped to say these things personally to you, and see your family after these many years. Honestly, I had not stayed in touch – the mores of society frowned on such for so many years, and we shared no common social events to even run into each other – and thus probably had not spoken to Cathy in 15 years. If it wasn't for my mother-in-law who taught with Cathy at George Jenkins, I probably would never have known of her cancer, which I learned of only less than a month ago, or her passing. Being in the midst of our most trying operational season in our corporation's 37 year history, I put off making contact because the on-line articles that I saw indicated that the cancer had been defeated. Being new to Facebook in the last couple of months and seeing that she had befriended everyone that we went to high school with, I looked forward to touching base with her after our busy season ended last week. Of course, I was stunned and saddened to receive another phone call from my mother-in-law on

Wednesday. Cathy had managed to keep tabs on me through one of my colleagues that knew her from First Presbyterian and that she would see on occasion at Anthony's Health Hut. Inexcusably, I did not show such diligence, and my opportunity to reach out to her was lost. One does not expect this at 39 or to learn someone had battled cancer for as long as she had. Please forgive me for my failings all of these years. It has been a humbling and bitter experience for me.

However, I write not solely out of catharsis, but to share a reflection of Cathy which has grown stronger to me through the years and has brought a smile to my face in the midst of sadness. I suppose this reflection was still true these last 15 years. From what I read on the internet in various places, I believe it was. As background to this comment, you might recall, our family's mission has been to increase Biblical awareness through pilgrimages to the lands of the Bible. The Bible refers to the Christian as a stranger, sojourner, and pilgrim during this life on our way to the true Promised Land. The concept of the pilgrim to me is one I live with on a daily basis. Chaucer wrote of various pilgrims that were on their way to Canterbury in the Canterbury Tales, singular people each with their own distinctive traits. In my profession, I have met and work with religious leaders from Armenian Orthodox to Joel Osteen and have met royalty, political leaders, and the like. I have had hundreds of employees, some have worked for us 25+ years, fired many others, have had some pass away, have had 3 embezzlers in various degrees and two commit suicide while in my employ. This does not even include working in the shifting sands of the Middle East for all these years where one must assume that one is being lied to or manipulated at all times.

In my pilgrimage here on this earth, Cathy will always be my shining example of sincerity amongst the thousands of people that I have met. If holiness is God's attribute that transcends all of His other attributes, then sincerity was God's transcending gift to Cathy. She was sincere in her schoolwork, her cheering, her friendships, her conversations, her smile, her faith, her avoidance of sin, or anything that resembled sin, and frankly any other trait that I can think of. There were no ulterior motives, nothing done for show, no pharisaical displays. All of us knew Cathy was different in a good way, but through the hormones, teenage peer pressure, worldly vanity, etc. we had no perspective to fully appreciate that sincerity. While I have been blessed with family members now who I consider Godly and sincere people, I have still never been so impressed with sincerity under fire as I saw with Cathy in our teenage years. It would have been so easy to have succumbed to the myriad temptations, vices or just have a plain grudge, but it just was never the case that I saw. To the "least" person in the class, she could communicate with and be their greatest friend – I still remember her warm greeting after my first class when I started at Evangel in the middle of the 8th grade year. She was ridiculed or despised behind her back by different people on many occasions – I am sure she knew that this happened as she was not naive – but just kept being that sincere person God created her to be. She never missed her weekly silent prayer time in Mrs. Braxton's classroom which surely was not the "cool" thing to be doing in high school. I could easily go on, but Cathy's sincerity during those years cannot be questioned, and to this day I have admired that attribute in her.

Years later and with a healthy dose of gray hair, it is hard to fathom all of the depravity of man that I have seen. With that, though, it is easy to remember, the very few flashes of Spirit-filled Christians on this pilgrimage of faith that I have met. Those people have surely been God-given to me, similar to the roll call of faith in Hebrews, that I might know Him more fully, even if I did not comprehend those examples and appreciate them as much as I should have when I was with them. This is the picture of Christ, and I am privileged to say that this has been revealed to me in Cathy those many years ago.

With such a strong family, church, and large number of friends, I know she did not lack in the love that was shown to her and for that I am grateful to the Lord. However, I do wish I could have told her the meaning of her sincere witness to me in those years as I had planned. But, I know that sincerity did not come about in a vacuum, and I appreciate now as a parent how difficult raising God-fearing children can be. Thanks for your diligence in raising Cathy and for sharing Cathy with us. I am pleased that I could at least share these memories with you. May God bless your memories, as He has mine, and the rest of your days of sojourning here. May Christ be your peace, your comfort, and your rest in this time.

Sincerely,

James (Jimmy) Ridgway

Beth Carter Photography

APPENDIX III ~ A LETTER FROM SELAH

Not long after our daughter Selah was born, having already gone to heaven, my sweet friend Pam Mutz gave me a gift including this card. Years prior, Pam's infant son drowned, so she knew the pain of the death of a child. She knew how to encourage, listen, pray, and love. This card was written to us, her parents, from Selah's perspective.

To Mom and Dad,

I know this is a sad Christmas for you without me, but I want you to know that Jesus is taking care of me and I have a front row seat to His birthday celebration!

He has told me about your love for me and shown me the bowl that contains your tears. Mommy and Daddy, did you know those will be changed into tears of joy?

It won't be long and I will be in your arms to love, hold, and perhaps even raise. I don't feel like an orphan at all because Jesus holds me all the time on His lap. He makes me laugh really hard, too. He even tells me stories about the two of you and that I am in your heart, especially when you sing and praise Him.

Isn't that amazing? So, just like you waited for me for nine months (or even longer), the day finally came for us to be together, and then...Jesus sent His angels and surprised me with the beautiful trip to Paradise. Oh mommy, I mean beautiful! Daddy, you would like the flight. Anyway, it will be just a little bit longer. Don't give up. We'll be together and as a family, I will see you face to face soon.... And Merry Christ-mas!

Love,

Selah Ann

XO

Cindy Lou Cleveland

QUIET STRENGTH

A TRUE STORY OF UNEXPECTED LOSS
AND UNEXPLAINABLE PEACE

Photo by Casey J. Cleveland

ABOUT THE AUTHOR

Cindy Lou Cleveland discovered her love for music as a child and her love for writing as an adult. In addition to being a worship leader and an author, Cindy Lou is a speaker at retreats, church services, and ministry events. She is married to her best friend Casey. They reside in Florida with their four boisterous blessings called boys. Their daughter Selah lives in heaven with Jesus.

www.CindyLouCleveland.com

RESTING LIFE
EDITING

YOUR CONTENT: PROFESSIONALLY PRESENTED	YOUR MESSAGE: CLEARLY COMMUNICATED
Flawless content	Thorough
Comprehensive analysis	Professional
Excellence and integrity	Affordable

ERIKA MATHEWS,
FREELANCE
EDITOR

WWW.RESTINGLIFE.COM

Made in the USA
Monee, IL
01 February 2020